Praying The Kingdom of Christ Come Now!
A Pattern for Everyone

BOOKS BY

KELAFO and SHALLAYWA Collie

Dr. Kelafo Z. Collie, M.D., D. DDIV, &
Dr. Shallaywa Collie, D.DIV, Ph.D.,

Majestic Priesthood Publications

Copyright ©2024 Dr. Kelafo Z. Collie, M.D., D.DIV, &
Dr. Shallaywa Collie, D.DIV, Ph.D., MBA

Praying The Kingdom of Christ Come Now!
ISBN **979-8-9906958-6-3**

www.kamgbahamas.com
www.kelafozcollie.com
www.shallaywa.com

Published by:
Majestic Priesthood Publication,
Freeport, Grand Bahama, Bahamas.
Email: mpppublications@gmail.com
1-242-727-2137

Printed in the United States of America

Summary of the Book

Praying the Kingdom of Jesus is more than a book — it is a **spiritual constitution** for those ready to confront darkness and establish divine order in the earth. With over **750 spiritually-charged declarations**, this book empowers the modern-day believer to:

- Break demonic assignments over the soul, body, and destiny

- Rule over territories and atmospheres by the authority of Jesus

- War against satanic princes in high places and regions of darkness

- Confront sexual perversion, false religion, drug addiction, and death

- Release the Kingdom of God into every realm: family, media, business, medicine, education, and government

- Pray with the governmental voice of Christ to enforce victory

"Praying the Kingdom of Jesus – Apostolic Declarations for Spiritual Dominion" is a revolutionary spiritual tool that combines biblical authority with prophetic declaration to empower believers to wage war in the spirit — and win.

This book contains **strategically designed Kingdom decrees** that empower the Church to:

- **Break** demonic strongholds over mind, body, will, emotions, and relationships.

- **Enforce** Christ's reign over systems of government, education, medicine, business, and culture.

- **Dismantle** satanic operations in second heaven realms, astral warfare, and spiritual gates.

- **Confront** the rise of false religion, deception, ancestral worship, sexual perversion, and death.

- **Rebuild** families, cities, and nations under apostolic truth and prophetic fire.

Each declaration is written with militant precision and spiritual boldness, equipping believers to speak as heaven's ambassadors in the earth. Whether you're confronting spiritual wickedness in your home, workplace, city, or nation, these declarations are designed to **shift atmospheres**, **restore righteousness**, and **advance the rule of Jesus Christ** with power.

This is not just a prayer book — it is a **Kingdom constitution** for a new era of spiritual warfare, prophetic intercession, and divine takeover. Every reader will come away with a renewed fire for holiness, a fresh understanding of spiritual government, and a sharpened tongue ready to legislate heaven's will.

The book is structured into organized sections, each with bold declarations that bring divine judgment to the enemy and manifest the will of the King. Every decree is an act of spiritual warfare, every section a blueprint for takeover, and every word an instrument of deliverance and glory.

This is a prophetic tool for apostolic reformation, citywide revival, and personal transformation.

> **"Thy Kingdom come. Thy will be done on earth as it is in heaven."**
> **– Matthew 6:10**
>
> **"And He shall reign forever and ever." – Revelation 11:15**
>
> **"The kingdoms of this world have become the kingdoms of our Lord and of His Christ, and He shall reign forever and ever." — Revelation 11:15**

Introduction

The Kingdom of Jesus Christ is not a theory, doctrine, or abstraction — it is the supreme, present, and advancing rule of the risen King, established in heaven and now enforced through His people on earth. When Jesus taught His disciples to pray, He declared, "Your Kingdom come, Your will be done on earth as it is in heaven" (Matthew 6:10). That command was not a poetic aspiration — it was a militant call to spiritual government.

This book is born from that command. It is a weaponized collection of apostolic decrees forged in prayer, seasoned by spiritual warfare, and sharpened by revelation. It is not a devotional for the timid or a mere encouragement for daily life. It is a prophetic arsenal for saints, intercessors, leaders, and watchmen who understand the urgency of enforcing Christ's dominion over every sphere of life.

These declarations confront strongholds and principalities that war against the Church, families, governments, cities, and the destinies of nations. They address the unseen realms, legislating the rule of Jesus over everything from the human soul to the gates of hell itself.

Inspired by the apostolic and prophetic tradition, these Kingdom decrees activate heaven's power to bind, loose, uproot, overthrow, plant, and rebuild (Jeremiah 1:10).

Whether you are a new believer growing in authority or a seasoned warrior contending for territory, this book equips you to pray — not reactively, but authoritatively. This is a Kingdom manual for those ready to move beyond survival into conquest.

Table of Contents

Pray Thy Kingdom Come

Prelude

Why These Prayers Matters Now

Praying the Kingdom of Jesus: A Scholarly Discourse on Matthew Chapter 6 and the Apostolic Mandate for Kingdom Prayer.

I. The Foundation of Kingdom Prayer: Matthew 6 and the Command of the King

When Jesus of Nazareth—the Messiah, Son of the Living God—walked among men, He did not merely teach ethics, perform miracles, or gather followers. He inaugurated a government. This divine government, called the Kingdom of God or the Kingdom of Heaven, is not confined to geography, ethnicity, or denomination. It is the eternal rulership of Christ breaking into time and space, calling all men everywhere to repent and submit to His rule.

In **Matthew 6:9–13**, Jesus delivers what has become known as the Lord's Prayer. However, this prayer is not a sentimental poem or spiritual mantra—it is a **constitutional decree**, a spiritual blueprint for every believer to understand the nature, structure, and mission of Kingdom-centered prayer:

> "Our Father who art in heaven, hallowed be thy name. *Thy Kingdom come. Thy will be done on earth, as it is in heaven.* Give us this day our daily bread. And forgive us our debts, as we forgive our debtors. And lead us not into temptation, but deliver us from evil. *For Thine is the Kingdom, and the power, and the glory, forever. Amen." (Matthew 6:9–13, KJV)

These words frame the **apostolic foundation for all Kingdom intercession.** Jesus was not merely telling us what to say, but how to pray—how to align the heart, voice, and authority of the believer with the agenda of heaven.

II. "Thy Kingdom Come": The Invocation of Governmental Rule

The phrase *"Thy Kingdom come"* is not a passive desire but a **militant declaration**. In ancient times, a kingdom could only expand through conquest. Jesus, therefore, calls His disciples to speak, live, and pray in such a way that heaven's government invades earth's rebellion. The Kingdom is not coming to take sides — it comes to take over.

Every declaration of *"Thy Kingdom come"* is a legal summons of heaven's jurisdiction over:

- Earthly systems of corruption and sin
- Demonic thrones, principalities, and territorial spirits
- Human rebellion and religious compromise
- Families, cities, nations, and every mountain of influence

This is not a generalized prayer; it is a **strategic, apostolic command** that births heaven's intervention in specific earthly realities.

When believers say, *"Thy will be done on earth as it is in heaven,"* they are **enforcing divine order** where demonic chaos exists. They are commanding the alignment of culture, government, sexuality, economics, education, and personal destiny with the standards of heaven.

III. "For Thine is the Kingdom, the Power, and the Glory": The Eternal Dominion of Christ

Jesus concludes the prayer by anchoring all intercession in the **absolute and unshakable dominion of the Father**: *"For Thine is the Kingdom, and the power, and the glory forever."* This triune declaration establishes:

- The **right of ownership** (*Thine is the Kingdom*)
- The **source of supernatural authority** (*Thine is the power*)
- The **objective of all things created** (*Thine is the glory*)

This divine doxology is not merely the end of a prayer—it is a **mandate for warfare**. The Kingdom of Jesus is eternal, and every enemy of that Kingdom must bow, retreat, or be overthrown.

IV. The Global Mandate: Preach the Kingdom Before the End Comes

Jesus' words in **Matthew 24:14** are clear:

> "And this gospel of the Kingdom shall be preached in all the world for a witness unto all nations; and then shall the end come."

This affirms that the **Gospel of the Kingdom**—not just a gospel of personal salvation, but of Kingdom rulership—must be proclaimed to every nation. No other message can complete the prophetic timeline. This means Kingdom prayers and apostolic decrees are not optional—they are the **engine of global transformation** and the prerequisite for the return of the King.

To preach the Kingdom is to challenge idols, systems, governments, false religions, and spiritual darkness. Therefore, every prayer that says *"Thy Kingdom come"* is a **declaration of war against the status quo**.

V. The Resistance Against Kingdom Advancement

The forces of darkness do not fear religious rituals or powerless prayers. What they fear is **Kingdom intercession**—the kind that legislates from the throne of Christ. Demons flee when believers declare with governmental authority, *"I release and declare the Kingdom of Jesus, His rule and reign..."*

The enemy will resist this. He will raise:

- False doctrines to obscure the Kingdom
- Political systems to silence the Church
- Cultural compromise to weaken holiness
- Occult power to seduce the people

But the prayers of the righteous will not be stopped. Kingdom prayer is not only intercession—it is **spiritual warfare, prophetic resistance, and heavenly invasion.**

VI. The Urgency of Daily Apostolic Prayer

Kingdom prayer is not occasional—it is essential. Jesus modeled continual communion with the Father, and Paul charged believers to "pray without ceasing." Apostolic declarations such as:

> "I release and declare the Kingdom of Jesus, His rule and reign over my mind, my body, my city, and my nation..."

...are not mere repetitions—they are **daily legal activations of heaven's reign.**

This is why every disciple of Jesus must become fluent in Kingdom decrees. Not only to guard their personal lives, but to partner with the Holy Spirit in **transforming cities, confronting darkness, and hastening the return of the Lord.**

The Kingdom must be prayed. The Kingdom must be preached. The Kingdom must be enforced.

> **"Let Your Kingdom come. Let Your will be done. For Yours is the Kingdom, the power, and the glory—forever."**

Amen.

These declarations are designed for spiritual warfare, deliverance, and the advancement of the Kingdom of God in every sphere of life and society.

PRAYING THE KINGDOM OF JESUS:

Pray
Without
Ceasing

Section One

Mind, Body, Soul, and Spirit (Declarations 1–20)

1. I release and declare the Kingdom of Jesus, His rule and reign over my mind—every thought is brought into obedience to Christ; I cast down imaginations, and bind mental torment, anxiety, and confusion.

2. I release and declare the Kingdom of Jesus, His rule and reign over my body—sickness, disease, fatigue, and demonic infirmity must go now by the authority of the blood of Jesus.

3. I release and declare the Kingdom of Jesus, His rule and reign over my soul—I am anchored in righteousness, my emotions are stabilized, and the fruit of the Spirit governs my desires.

4. I release and declare the Kingdom of Jesus, His rule and reign over my spirit—I walk in divine alignment, Holy Spirit-filled, and sensitive to the voice of the Lord.

5. I release and declare the Kingdom of Jesus, His rule and reign over every stronghold in my mind—I bind the spirits of fear, depression, double-mindedness, and torment in Jesus' name.

6. I release and declare the Kingdom of Jesus, His rule and reign to flood my thought life with divine strategies and creative insight.

7. I release and declare the Kingdom of Jesus, His rule and reign to break every generational curse affecting my physical health.

8. I release and declare the Kingdom of Jesus, His rule and reign to restore my soul from past trauma, abuse, and rejection.

9. I release and declare the Kingdom of Jesus, His rule and reign to open my spirit to deeper encounters with God.

10. I release and declare the Kingdom of Jesus, His rule and reign to dismantle every altar of demonic mental oppression.

11. I release and declare the Kingdom of Jesus, His rule and reign over my brain chemistry — chemical imbalances are corrected now by divine order.

12. I release and declare the Kingdom of Jesus, His rule and reign to consume all fatigue, weariness, and exhaustion.

13. I release and declare the Kingdom of Jesus, His rule and reign to command every demon hiding in my emotions to be exposed and expelled.

14. I release and declare the Kingdom of Jesus, His rule and reign to align my soul with heaven's rhythms and heavenly joy.

15. I release and declare the Kingdom of Jesus, His rule and reign to break the spirit of heaviness and release garments of praise.

16. I release and declare the Kingdom of Jesus, His rule and reign to command all spirits of addiction, lust, and bondage to flee.

17. I release and declare the Kingdom of Jesus, His rule and reign to release angelic warfare over my inner man.

18. I release and declare the Kingdom of Jesus, His rule and reign to renew my youth and repair every damaged cell and organ.

19. I release and declare the Kingdom of Jesus, His rule and reign to illuminate my spirit with prophetic light and truth.

20. I release and declare the Kingdom of Jesus, His rule and reign to establish unshakable peace in my body, soul, and spirit.

Section Two

Family and Marriage (Declarations 21–40)

21. I release and declare the Kingdom of Jesus, His rule and reign over my household—as for me and my house, we will serve the Lord; every spirit of strife, rebellion, and division is bound.

22. I release and declare the Kingdom of Jesus, His rule and reign over my marriage—let love, honor, and covenantal faithfulness arise; I cancel every demonic assignment sent to sabotage my union.

23. I release and declare the Kingdom of Jesus, His rule and reign to cover my children—they are protected, preserved, and marked for the purposes of God.

24. I release and declare the Kingdom of Jesus, His rule and reign to expose and destroy every generational curse operating in my family line.

25. I release and declare the Kingdom of Jesus, His rule and reign to bind the spirits of divorce, adultery, and broken covenants in my bloodline.

26. I release and declare the Kingdom of Jesus, His rule and reign to restore lost communication and understanding between spouses and family members.

27. I release and declare the Kingdom of Jesus, His rule and reign to call forth prodigal sons and daughters from rebellion into divine purpose.

28. I release and declare the Kingdom of Jesus, His rule and reign to sanctify my home with peace, worship, and prophetic intercession.

29. I release and declare the Kingdom of Jesus, His rule and reign to cause husbands to love their wives as Christ loves the Church, and wives to honor their husbands with grace.

30. I release and declare the Kingdom of Jesus, His rule and reign to drive out spirits of abuse, manipulation, and control from my marriage and family.

31. I release and declare the Kingdom of Jesus, His rule and reign to make my children wise, strong in the Spirit, and filled with divine favor.

32. I release and declare the Kingdom of Jesus, His rule and reign to dismantle every word curse, hex, or incantation spoken over my family.

33. I release and declare the Kingdom of Jesus, His rule and reign to set divine order in my household, where Christ is the head and peace is our portion.

34. I release and declare the Kingdom of Jesus, His rule and reign to stir up priestly leadership in every man and prophetic discernment in every woman.

35. I release and declare the Kingdom of Jesus, His rule and reign to make my family a witness of Kingdom culture and heavenly authority.

36. I release and declare the Kingdom of Jesus, His rule and reign to guard my home with angelic hosts and walls of fire.

37. I release and declare the Kingdom of Jesus, His rule and reign to bring healing from broken marriages and supernatural restoration of love.

38. I release and declare the Kingdom of Jesus, His rule and reign to cause my family line to serve in the Kingdom with signs, wonders, and miracles.

39. I release and declare the Kingdom of Jesus, His rule and reign to break the grip of idolatry, false religion, and lukewarmness in my family.

40. I release and declare the Kingdom of Jesus, His rule and reign to raise up legacy, lineage, and leadership for the generations to come.

Section Three

Cities, Nations, and Government (Declarations 41–60)

41. I release and declare the Kingdom of Jesus, His rule and reign over my city — let righteousness exalt this land; every spirit of violence, corruption, and bloodshed is bound and cast out.

42. I release and declare the Kingdom of Jesus, His rule and reign over this nation — let godly governance arise and every demonic throne of wickedness be overturned.

43. I release and declare the Kingdom of Jesus, His rule and reign over our gates — every gate of influence (media, politics, commerce, culture) shall be secured by Kingdom watchmen.

44. I release and declare the Kingdom of Jesus, His rule and reign over our elected officials — remove the ungodly and raise up leaders after Your heart.

45. I release and declare the Kingdom of Jesus, His rule and reign to displace spirits of Jezebel, Leviathan, and witchcraft from the halls of governance.

46. I release and declare the Kingdom of Jesus, His rule and reign to establish apostolic order and justice in the judiciary and legal systems.

47. I release and declare the Kingdom of Jesus, His rule and reign to break the power of mammon and greed over national economies.

48. I release and declare the Kingdom of Jesus, His rule and reign over every governmental mountain with truth, equity, and integrity.

49. I release and declare the Kingdom of Jesus, His rule and reign over the military—let divine protection, wisdom, and righteousness rest on those who defend the land.

50. I release and declare the Kingdom of Jesus, His rule and reign to dismantle every occult altar and hidden agenda fueling unrest, division, and political strife.

51. I release and declare the Kingdom of Jesus, His rule and reign to appoint Daniels and Josephs to advise and influence heads of state.

52. I release and declare the Kingdom of Jesus, His rule and reign over police forces and military branches—no more abuse, racism, or lawlessness in authority.

53. I release and declare the Kingdom of Jesus, His rule and reign to uproot human trafficking networks and rescue the oppressed.

54. I release and declare the Kingdom of Jesus, His rule and reign over national borders—let peace be our walls and salvation our gates.

55. I release and declare the Kingdom of Jesus, His rule and reign to release angelic armies over the nation's capital, government centers, and civic buildings.

56. I release and declare the Kingdom of Jesus, His rule and reign to break demonic alliances, secret societies, and globalist conspiracies that resist Christ.

57. I release and declare the Kingdom of Jesus, His rule and reign to fill every court, mayoral office, senate, parliament, and presidential seat with the fear of the Lord.

58. I release and declare the Kingdom of Jesus, His rule and reign over national educational policies, economic strategies, and healthcare reform.

59. I release and declare the Kingdom of Jesus, His rule and reign to establish global revival and align the nations with the Gospel of the Kingdom.

60. I release and declare the Kingdom of Jesus, His rule and reign to cause every knee in high places to bow and confess that Jesus is Lord.

Section *Four*

Business, Finance, and the Marketplace (Declarations 61–92)

61. I release and declare the Kingdom of Jesus, His rule and reign over the business world—let righteous entrepreneurship arise and displace every corrupt enterprise.

62. I release and declare the Kingdom of Jesus, His rule and reign over the financial systems of this world—I bind the spirit of mammon and loose Kingdom wealth and stewardship.

63. I release and declare the Kingdom of Jesus, His rule and reign to raise up Kingdom financiers who fund the Gospel, feed the hungry, and break poverty cycles.

64. I release and declare the Kingdom of Jesus, His rule and reign over banks, stocks, investments, and markets—let divine wisdom govern every transaction.

65. I release and declare the Kingdom of Jesus, His rule and reign to expose fraudulent schemes, money laundering, and economic oppression.

66. I release and declare the Kingdom of Jesus, His rule and reign to break every generational curse of debt, lack, and financial mismanagement.

67. I release and declare the Kingdom of Jesus, His rule and reign over my own finances—I am a lender, not a borrower, a giver, not a beggar.

68. I release and declare the Kingdom of Jesus, His rule and reign over business owners and entrepreneurs—ignite vision, discipline, and divine success.

69. I release and declare the Kingdom of Jesus, His rule and reign to bring supernatural provision and overflow to Kingdom builders.

70. I release and declare the Kingdom of Jesus, His rule and reign to dismantle monopolies and systems that suppress small businesses and local economies.

71. I release and declare the Kingdom of Jesus, His rule and reign to open gates of commerce for Kingdom-minded entrepreneurs in every nation.

72. I release and declare the Kingdom of Jesus, His rule and reign to break the power of greed, exploitation, and unjust labor systems.

73. I release and declare the Kingdom of Jesus, His rule and reign to release financial angels to war on behalf of stalled Kingdom visions.

74. I release and declare the Kingdom of Jesus, His rule and reign to make Christian business leaders apostles in the marketplace.

75. I release and declare the Kingdom of Jesus, His rule and reign to crush demonic altars in boardrooms, financial districts, and global economic summits.

76. I release and declare the Kingdom of Jesus, His rule and reign to pour out divine strategies for innovation, impact, and global expansion.

77. I release and declare the Kingdom of Jesus, His rule and reign to raise up Christian CEOs who lead with righteousness and prophetic boldness.

78. I release and declare the Kingdom of Jesus, His rule and reign to sanctify income streams, cancel financial curses, and release breakthrough.

79. I release and declare the Kingdom of Jesus, His rule and reign over corporate mergers, partnerships, and board decisions — let God's will be established.

80. I release and declare the Kingdom of Jesus, His rule and reign to release Joseph anointings — economic saviors who preserve nations in famine.

81. I release and declare the Kingdom of Jesus, His rule and reign to empower Christian entrepreneurs with supernatural strategy and market dominance.

82. I release and declare the Kingdom of Jesus, His rule and reign to sanctify commercial real estate, tech industries, and investment portfolios.

83. I release and declare the Kingdom of Jesus, His rule and reign to expose secret covenants with mammon and establish a wealth transfer to the righteous.

84. I release and declare the Kingdom of Jesus, His rule and reign to create debt-free enterprises that fund Kingdom missions and social reform.

85. I release and declare the Kingdom of Jesus, His rule and reign to destroy the power of economic racism, exploitation, and systemic injustice.

86. I release and declare the Kingdom of Jesus, His rule and reign to raise up apostolic voices in the marketplace who govern in righteousness.

87. I release and declare the Kingdom of Jesus, His rule and reign to activate spiritual gifts in business leaders — dream interpretation, wisdom, and discernment.

88. I release and declare the Kingdom of Jesus, His rule and reign to release financial revival in cities, nations, and regions that have been in drought.

89. I release and declare the Kingdom of Jesus, His rule and reign to build a remnant economy that is independent of Babylonian systems.

90. I release and declare the Kingdom of Jesus, His rule and reign to break financial witchcraft, unjust contracts, and blood money.

91. I release and declare the Kingdom of Jesus, His rule and reign to recover every stolen inheritance, withheld wage, and delayed promise.

92. I release and declare the Kingdom of Jesus, His rule and reign to establish Kingdom banks, trade hubs, and cooperative economies.

Section *Five*

Education, Medicine, Arts, and Entertainment (Declarations 93-148)

Education and Academics

93. I release and declare the Kingdom of Jesus, His rule and reign over the education system—every institution, from preschool to university, shall be reformed by truth and righteousness.

94. I release and declare the Kingdom of Jesus, His rule and reign over teachers and administrators—raise up educators with wisdom, compassion, and fear of the Lord.

95. I release and declare the Kingdom of Jesus, His rule and reign to remove every demonic curriculum, ungodly agenda, and antichrist ideology from our schools.

96. I release and declare the Kingdom of Jesus, His rule and reign to anoint students with supernatural intelligence, creativity, and boldness to stand for truth.

97. I release and declare the Kingdom of Jesus, His rule and reign to restore prayer, scripture, and moral excellence in classrooms across the nations.

98. I release and declare the Kingdom of Jesus, His rule and reign over educational policies—let reform, revival, and revelation be written into law.

99. I release and declare the Kingdom of Jesus, His rule and reign to break the stronghold of indoctrination, perversion, and academic elitism.

100. I release and declare the Kingdom of Jesus, His rule and reign to appoint Kingdom-minded leaders in every school board and academic council.

101. I release and declare the Kingdom of Jesus, His rule and reign to reform educational institutions into centers of truth, integrity, and divine purpose.

102. I release and declare the Kingdom of Jesus, His rule and reign to awaken the fear of the Lord in every educator, professor, and curriculum designer.

103. I release and declare the Kingdom of Jesus, His rule and reign over school funding—let it be just, sufficient, and free from political manipulation.

104. I release and declare the Kingdom of Jesus, His rule and reign to expose and dismantle doctrines of demons embedded in academic materials.

105. I release and declare the Kingdom of Jesus, His rule and reign to raise up Kingdom intercessors who pray over every school district, principal, and teacher.

106. I release and declare the Kingdom of Jesus, His rule and reign to saturate homeschool movements with anointed content and divine favor.

107. I release and declare the Kingdom of Jesus, His rule and reign to impart divine dreams and visions to young learners that will guide them in destiny.

108. I release and declare the Kingdom of Jesus, His rule and reign to anoint counselors, chaplains, and mentors to shepherd students with discernment and compassion.

109. I release and declare the Kingdom of Jesus, His rule and reign to release bold young voices who speak truth and carry the fire of revival in academic halls.

110. I release and declare the Kingdom of Jesus, His rule and reign to break every agenda of premature sexualization and gender confusion in education.

111. I release and declare the Kingdom of Jesus, His rule and reign to ignite revival fires in public, private, and online schools across the globe.

112. I release and declare the Kingdom of Jesus, His rule and reign to raise up Kingdom reformers who will write, teach, and administrate under divine wisdom.

Medicine and Healthcare

113. I release and declare the Kingdom of Jesus, His rule and reign over the medical and healthcare industries — healing, compassion, and justice shall prevail.

114. I release and declare the Kingdom of Jesus, His rule and reign to break the grip of pharmaceutical idolatry, malpractice, and greed in the health sector.

115. I release and declare the Kingdom of Jesus, His rule and reign to raise up Holy Spirit-filled doctors, nurses, and researchers led by divine wisdom.

116. I release and declare the Kingdom of Jesus, His rule and reign to dismantle the spirit of infirmity and release the healing power of Jehovah Rapha.

117. I release and declare the Kingdom of Jesus, His rule and reign over public health policy — let righteousness and truth replace deception and corruption.

118. I release and declare the Kingdom of Jesus, His rule and reign to ignite revival in hospitals, clinics, and care centers — let miracles become standard.

119. I release and declare the Kingdom of Jesus, His rule and reign to establish healing centers where miracles, science, and compassion converge.

120.	I release and declare the Kingdom of Jesus, His rule and reign to raise up apostolic medical missionaries with cures and Holy Spirit revelation.

121.	I release and declare the Kingdom of Jesus, His rule and reign to tear down altars of pharmakeia and demonic pharmaceutical manipulation.

122.	I release and declare the Kingdom of Jesus, His rule and reign to fund hospitals that honor life, dignity, and God's design.

123.	I release and declare the Kingdom of Jesus, His rule and reign to cleanse the medical field of hidden abortion agendas and culture of death.

124.	I release and declare the Kingdom of Jesus, His rule and reign to sanctify every operating room, laboratory, and medical conference.

125.	I release and declare the Kingdom of Jesus, His rule and reign to give doctors prophetic insight into undiscovered cures and hidden conditions.

126.	I release and declare the Kingdom of Jesus, His rule and reign to redeem health systems from corporate greed and patient exploitation.

127.	I release and declare the Kingdom of Jesus, His rule and reign to break the demonic spirit of fear that drives medical decisions and diagnoses.

128.	I release and declare the Kingdom of Jesus, His rule and reign to heal trauma in healthcare workers and renew their call to serve.

129.	I release and declare the Kingdom of Jesus, His rule and reign to fill every ambulance, ER, and ICU with angelic hosts.

130.	I release and declare the Kingdom of Jesus, His rule and reign to eradicate plagues, epidemics, and bioengineered diseases.

Music, Arts, and Entertainment

131. I release and declare the Kingdom of Jesus, His rule and reign over the music industry — purify the sound, redeem the artists, and dethrone idols.

132. I release and declare the Kingdom of Jesus, His rule and reign to raise up psalmists, minstrels, and worshippers who release heavenly frequencies on earth.

133. I release and declare the Kingdom of Jesus, His rule and reign over film, television, and digital platforms — let Kingdom narratives dominate the screen.

134. I release and declare the Kingdom of Jesus, His rule and reign to break the control of perversion, witchcraft, and violence in entertainment.

135. I release and declare the Kingdom of Jesus, His rule and reign to anoint Christian artists, actors, and creators to shine as lights in dark places.

136. I release and declare the Kingdom of Jesus, His rule and reign to take back the airwaves, platforms, and studios for the glory of God.

137. I release and declare the Kingdom of Jesus, His rule and reign to break the power of the spirit of Baal and Molech from media and entertainment.

138. I release and declare the Kingdom of Jesus, His rule and reign to raise up prophetic musicians who carry the sound of heaven.

139. I release and declare the Kingdom of Jesus, His rule and reign to remove every agent of darkness behind global music labels and streaming platforms.

140. I release and declare the Kingdom of Jesus, His rule and reign to empower visual artists to prophesy through their creativity and design.

141. I release and declare the Kingdom of Jesus, His rule and reign to revive purity in storytelling, screenwriting, and narrative creation.

142. I release and declare the Kingdom of Jesus, His rule and reign to open international doors for Kingdom films, albums, and creative content.

143. I release and declare the Kingdom of Jesus, His rule and reign to silence the voices of seduction, rebellion, and mockery in the arts.

144. I release and declare the Kingdom of Jesus, His rule and reign to fund Christian creatives with abundance for global impact.

145. I release and declare the Kingdom of Jesus, His rule and reign to disrupt the entertainment industry with holy conviction and repentance.

146. I release and declare the Kingdom of Jesus, His rule and reign to cleanse awards shows, festivals, and media summits of demonic worship.

147. I release and declare the Kingdom of Jesus, His rule and reign to break addiction to ungodly content and restore delight in holy entertainment.

148. I release and declare the Kingdom of Jesus, His rule and reign to establish a new era of entertainment that exalts Christ and His Kingdom.

Intercession Is the Key

Section Six

The Will (Declarations 149-163)

149. I release and declare the Kingdom of Jesus, His rule and reign over my will—let every choice align with the perfect will of God.

150. I release and declare the Kingdom of Jesus, His rule and reign to crush rebellion, stubbornness, and the refusal to yield to divine direction.

151. I release and declare the Kingdom of Jesus, His rule and reign to fortify my will with Kingdom resolve and spiritual determination.

152. I release and declare the Kingdom of Jesus, His rule and reign to destroy every ungodly soul tie that weakens my ability to say no to sin.

153. I release and declare the Kingdom of Jesus, His rule and reign to make my will submitted, surrendered, and strengthened in Christ.

154. I release and declare the Kingdom of Jesus, His rule and reign to deliver me from the spirit of passivity and spiritual laziness.

155. I release and declare the Kingdom of Jesus, His rule and reign to renew my decision-making with discernment, timing, and obedience.

156. I release and declare the Kingdom of Jesus, His rule and reign to align my ambitions with the desires of heaven.

157. I release and declare the Kingdom of Jesus, His rule and reign to give me boldness to act when God says move.

158. I release and declare the Kingdom of Jesus, His rule and reign to dismantle all manipulative influences trying to dominate my choices.

159. I release and declare the Kingdom of Jesus, His rule and reign to reignite spiritual hunger and holy drive in my inner man.

160. I release and declare the Kingdom of Jesus, His rule and reign to release grace to finish what I start and to stay faithful to my calling.

161. I release and declare the Kingdom of Jesus, His rule and reign to break the spirit of confusion and paralysis in decision-making.

162. I release and declare the Kingdom of Jesus, His rule and reign to cause my will to chase after purpose, not popularity.

163. I release and declare the Kingdom of Jesus, His rule and reign to declare divine victory over every battle in my will.

Section Seven

Emotions (Declarations 164-178)

164. I release and declare the Kingdom of Jesus, His rule and reign over my emotions—every wave of anxiety, sadness, and rage is subdued by the Prince of Peace.

165. I release and declare the Kingdom of Jesus, His rule and reign to heal wounds from emotional trauma, abuse, and rejection.

166. I release and declare the Kingdom of Jesus, His rule and reign to restore joy where sorrow has made its home.

167. I release and declare the Kingdom of Jesus, His rule and reign to dismantle emotional manipulation and false empathy used to control others.

168. I release and declare the Kingdom of Jesus, His rule and reign to uproot bitterness, unforgiveness, and emotional instability.

169. I release and declare the Kingdom of Jesus, His rule and reign to stabilize every mood swing and bring my soul into divine balance.

170. I release and declare the Kingdom of Jesus, His rule and reign to baptize my emotions with holy fire and Kingdom passion.

171. I release and declare the Kingdom of Jesus, His rule and reign to break the influence of media, trauma, and words that have distorted how I feel.

172. I release and declare the Kingdom of Jesus, His rule and reign to wash my emotions with the water of the Word.

173. I release and declare the Kingdom of Jesus, His rule and reign to anchor my heart in eternal hope, not circumstantial happiness.

174. I release and declare the Kingdom of Jesus, His rule and reign to command the storms of rage, depression, and grief to be still.

175. I release and declare the Kingdom of Jesus, His rule and reign to purify my affections and align my feelings with His truth.

176. I release and declare the Kingdom of Jesus, His rule and reign to break the power of emotional trauma passed through generations.

177. I release and declare the Kingdom of Jesus, His rule and reign to cultivate emotional intelligence that is Holy Spirit-led.

178. I release and declare the Kingdom of Jesus, His rule and reign to pour the oil of gladness where the spirit of heaviness once ruled.

Section Eight

Desires and Sexual Desires (Declarations 179-193)

179. I release and declare the Kingdom of Jesus, His rule and reign over every desire of my heart—let my longings be purified and redirected toward righteousness.

180. I release and declare the Kingdom of Jesus, His rule and reign to sanctify my passions, dreams, and personal ambitions under His will.

181. I release and declare the Kingdom of Jesus, His rule and reign to sever all ungodly cravings, fleshly obsessions, and counterfeit fulfillments.

182. I release and declare the Kingdom of Jesus, His rule and reign over my sexual desires—let them be holy, covenant-bound, and Spirit-governed.

183. I release and declare the Kingdom of Jesus, His rule and reign to break every soul tie formed through lust, fornication, adultery, or pornography.

184. I release and declare the Kingdom of Jesus, His rule and reign to cleanse my mind and body from every sexual defilement.

185. I release and declare the Kingdom of Jesus, His rule and reign to restore purity, passion, and purpose to marital intimacy.

186. I release and declare the Kingdom of Jesus, His rule and reign to destroy every altar of perversion, seduction, and gender confusion.

187. I release and declare the Kingdom of Jesus, His rule and reign to rewire desires that have been shaped by abuse, addiction, or demonic exposure.

188. I release and declare the Kingdom of Jesus, His rule and reign to guard my eyes, ears, and heart from lustful imagery and seducing spirits.

189. I release and declare the Kingdom of Jesus, His rule and reign to bring wholeness to my sexual identity as designed by God.

190. I release and declare the Kingdom of Jesus, His rule and reign to transform longing into intimacy with Christ rather than unhealthy attachments.

191. I release and declare the Kingdom of Jesus, His rule and reign to break the spirit of loneliness that drives unhealthy sexual desire.

192. I release and declare the Kingdom of Jesus, His rule and reign to anoint Kingdom marriages with holy desire, honor, and delight.

193. I release and declare the Kingdom of Jesus, His rule and reign to consume every hidden lust, secret sin, and unspoken addiction with His holy fire.

Section Nine

Creativity (Declarations 194-208)

194. I release and declare the Kingdom of Jesus, His rule and reign over my creative gifts — let divine inspiration flow without restriction.

195. I release and declare the Kingdom of Jesus, His rule and reign to unlock dormant talents, skills, and artistic expressions for Kingdom impact.

196. I release and declare the Kingdom of Jesus, His rule and reign to break the spirit of fear and perfectionism that hinders creative release.

197. I release and declare the Kingdom of Jesus, His rule and reign over my imagination — let it be sanctified and used for divine innovation.

198. I release and declare the Kingdom of Jesus, His rule and reign to raise up prophetic creatives who release Heaven through music, art, writing, and media.

199. I release and declare the Kingdom of Jesus, His rule and reign to download divine blueprints, designs, and solutions through Holy Spirit inspiration.

200. I release and declare the Kingdom of Jesus, His rule and reign to dismantle creative blocks, procrastination, and comparison.

201. I release and declare the Kingdom of Jesus, His rule and reign over every creative endeavor — let it glorify God and advance His Kingdom.

202. I release and declare the Kingdom of Jesus, His rule and reign to cleanse my creativity from demonic contamination and worldly compromise.

203. I release and declare the Kingdom of Jesus, His rule and reign to multiply the impact of Kingdom-authored books, films, and artistic works.

204. I release and declare the Kingdom of Jesus, His rule and reign to release joy and prophetic flow in every act of creation.

205. I release and declare the Kingdom of Jesus, His rule and reign to raise up creative apostles and reformers in every sphere of influence.

206. I release and declare the Kingdom of Jesus, His rule and reign to silence every voice that says I am not creative — my creativity is redeemed and commissioned.

207. I release and declare the Kingdom of Jesus, His rule and reign to birth art that delivers, heals, and sets captives free.

208. I release and declare the Kingdom of Jesus, His rule and reign to bring revival to the arts — let the Church lead the cultural conversation again.

Section *Ten*

Finances (Declarations 209-223)

209. I release and declare the Kingdom of Jesus, His rule and reign over my finances—let every dollar serve divine purpose.

210. I release and declare the Kingdom of Jesus, His rule and reign to break cycles of lack, poverty, and financial instability.

211. I release and declare the Kingdom of Jesus, His rule and reign to rebuke the devourer and release supernatural provision in my storehouses.

212. I release and declare the Kingdom of Jesus, His rule and reign to release prosperity with purpose, and wealth with wisdom.

213. I release and declare the Kingdom of Jesus, His rule and reign to expose and close doors of financial compromise and unrighteous gain.

214. I release and declare the Kingdom of Jesus, His rule and reign to activate radical generosity and multiply my seed for sowing.

215. I release and declare the Kingdom of Jesus, His rule and reign to cancel debt, erase burdens, and unlock new streams of income.

216. I release and declare the Kingdom of Jesus, His rule and reign over financial agreements, contracts, and negotiations—let them align with Kingdom justice.

217. I release and declare the Kingdom of Jesus, His rule and reign to crown God-fearing entrepreneurs and faithful stewards with abundance.

218. I release and declare the Kingdom of Jesus, His rule and reign to expose and destroy financial witchcraft, curses, and mammon-driven systems.

219. I release and declare the Kingdom of Jesus, His rule and reign to raise up end-time financiers who will fund revival and transformation.

220. I release and declare the Kingdom of Jesus, His rule and reign to bring Kingdom order to my spending, saving, and giving.

221. I release and declare the Kingdom of Jesus, His rule and reign to restore stolen inheritances and delayed promotions.

222. I release and declare the Kingdom of Jesus, His rule and reign to plant me in an economy that is not shaken by the systems of Babylon.

223. I release and declare the Kingdom of Jesus, His rule and reign to fill my hands with resources and my heart with compassion.

PRAY
THY
KINGDOM
COME

Section Eleven

Interpersonal Relationships (Declarations 224-238)

224. I release and declare the Kingdom of Jesus, His rule and reign over every relationship in my life — let divine alignment replace demonic entanglement.

225. I release and declare the Kingdom of Jesus, His rule and reign to sever toxic ties, manipulative connections, and soul-draining relationships.

226. I release and declare the Kingdom of Jesus, His rule and reign to surround me with covenant relationships that sharpen, strengthen, and stretch me.

227. I release and declare the Kingdom of Jesus, His rule and reign to expose hidden enemies posing as friends, and to bring separation with peace.

228. I release and declare the Kingdom of Jesus, His rule and reign to restore love, honor, and accountability in every godly relationship.

229. I release and declare the Kingdom of Jesus, His rule and reign to bind the spirit of offense, miscommunication, and relational sabotage.

230. I release and declare the Kingdom of Jesus, His rule and reign to break cycles of relational betrayal, mistrust, and rejection.

231. I release and declare the Kingdom of Jesus, His rule and reign to connect me with those who carry the keys to my next season.

232. I release and declare the Kingdom of Jesus, His rule and reign to cultivate honesty, forgiveness, and mutual edification in every connection.

233. I release and declare the Kingdom of Jesus, His rule and reign to reconcile estranged relationships that still carry Kingdom purpose.

234. I release and declare the Kingdom of Jesus, His rule and reign to destroy demonic wedges placed between family, leaders, and spiritual kin.

235. I release and declare the Kingdom of Jesus, His rule and reign to stir intercession, grace, and discernment within my relational circles.

236. I release and declare the Kingdom of Jesus, His rule and reign to bless me with mentors, fathers, mothers, and wise counsel.

237. I release and declare the Kingdom of Jesus, His rule and reign to bind loyalty, trust, and truth to every divine connection.

238. I release and declare the Kingdom of Jesus, His rule and reign to bring Kingdom order to the people I walk with, work with, and war with.

Section Twelve

Friendships (Declarations 239-253)

239. I release and declare the Kingdom of Jesus, His rule and reign over all my friendships—let them be holy, life-giving, and anchored in covenant.

240. I release and declare the Kingdom of Jesus, His rule and reign to remove false friends, secret rivals, and parasitic companions.

241. I release and declare the Kingdom of Jesus, His rule and reign to bless me with friends who fear God, speak truth, and walk in integrity.

242. I release and declare the Kingdom of Jesus, His rule and reign to restore friendships lost to offense, immaturity, or misunderstanding.

243. I release and declare the Kingdom of Jesus, His rule and reign to break the influence of betrayal, envy, and sabotage in my friendships.

244. I release and declare the Kingdom of Jesus, His rule and reign to multiply the strength of Kingdom friendships in this season.

245. I release and declare the Kingdom of Jesus, His rule and reign to release divine friendships that are purpose-driven and destiny-accelerating.

246. I release and declare the Kingdom of Jesus, His rule and reign to protect my friendships from gossip, assumption, and division.

247. I release and declare the Kingdom of Jesus, His rule and reign to elevate my friendships from surface-level to Spirit-led.

248. I release and declare the Kingdom of Jesus, His rule and reign to bring healing to wounds caused by broken trust.

249. I release and declare the Kingdom of Jesus, His rule and reign to make my presence life-giving and my counsel wise in the lives of my friends.

250. I release and declare the Kingdom of Jesus, His rule and reign to raise up intercessory friendships that cover me in prayer and warfare.

251. I release and declare the Kingdom of Jesus, His rule and reign to set boundaries in friendships that preserve holiness and honor.

252. I release and declare the Kingdom of Jesus, His rule and reign to create friendships that reflect heaven's community and Christ's love.

253. I release and declare the Kingdom of Jesus, His rule and reign to draw my friends and I closer to the cross, not the crowd.

Section Thirteen

Business Transactions (Declarations 254-268)

254. I release and declare the Kingdom of Jesus, His rule and reign over every business transaction — let righteousness, equity, and integrity govern each decision.

255. I release and declare the Kingdom of Jesus, His rule and reign to destroy every hidden trap, deceptive deal, and demonic entanglement in business.

256. I release and declare the Kingdom of Jesus, His rule and reign to grant me divine insight in contracts, investments, and partnerships.

257. I release and declare the Kingdom of Jesus, His rule and reign to surround my business dealings with favor, protection, and angelic intervention.

258. I release and declare the Kingdom of Jesus, His rule and reign to remove every Jezebel, Balaam, or Judas spirit from my business sphere.

259. I release and declare the Kingdom of Jesus, His rule and reign to attract trustworthy clients, vendors, and partners aligned with Kingdom values.

260. I release and declare the Kingdom of Jesus, His rule and reign to break the power of manipulation, bribery, and coercion in every negotiation.

261. I release and declare the Kingdom of Jesus, His rule and reign to bring supernatural multiplication and abundance through ethical transactions.

262. I release and declare the Kingdom of Jesus, His rule and reign to guard my business deals with wisdom, discernment, and prophetic insight.

263. I release and declare the Kingdom of Jesus, His rule and reign to unlock hidden opportunities and remove delays in business processes.

264. I release and declare the Kingdom of Jesus, His rule and reign to redeem every past failure and transform it into a future platform.

265. I release and declare the Kingdom of Jesus, His rule and reign to release Joseph-level strategy and Daniel-level excellence in all transactions.

266. I release and declare the Kingdom of Jesus, His rule and reign to expose unethical practices and cause them to be replaced with holy standards.

267. I release and declare the Kingdom of Jesus, His rule and reign to birth Kingdom-minded corporations that disciple nations through righteous wealth.

268. I release and declare the Kingdom of Jesus, His rule and reign to seal every transaction in the blood of Jesus and secure it under divine authority.

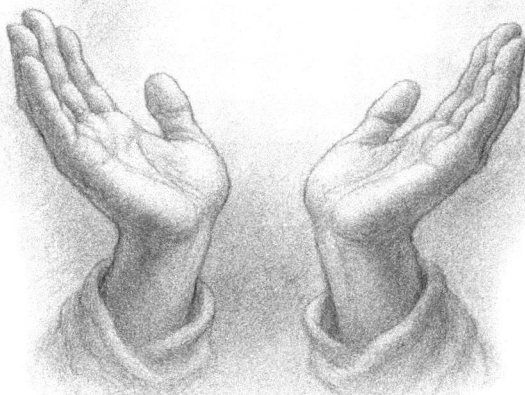

You are entering a powerful realm of **cosmic spiritual warfare**—*aligning creation and celestial realms under the* **rule and reign of Jesus Christ**.

Section *Fourteen*

The Sun, Moon, Stars, and Celestial Bodies (Declarations 269-288)

269. I release and declare the Kingdom of Jesus, His rule and reign over the sun—let it shine in alignment with divine glory and not empower any witchcraft.

270. I release and declare the Kingdom of Jesus, His rule and reign over the moon—every lunar cycle shall serve God's seasons and not be used for darkness.

271. I release and declare the Kingdom of Jesus, His rule and reign over the stars—let no astrologer, sorcerer, or diviner use them for evil.

272. I release and declare the Kingdom of Jesus, His rule and reign to dismantle all satanic altars built under the stars.

273. I release and declare the Kingdom of Jesus, His rule and reign to reclaim the heavens for righteous signs, seasons, and prophetic timelines.

274. I release and declare the Kingdom of Jesus, His rule and reign over every constellation—no demonic name shall hold dominion in the sky.

275. I release and declare the Kingdom of Jesus, His rule and reign to silence all astral projections and demonic rituals directed through heavenly bodies.

276. I release and declare the Kingdom of Jesus, His rule and reign to shatter demonic portals built around equinoxes, eclipses, and solstices.

277. I release and declare the Kingdom of Jesus, His rule and reign over the firmament—let it respond only to the voice of God.

278. I release and declare the Kingdom of Jesus, His rule and reign to arrest spirits operating through solar flares, planetary alignments, and cosmic manipulation.

279. I release and declare the Kingdom of Jesus, His rule and reign to cleanse the heavens of every satanic frequency, sound, and vibration.

280. I release and declare the Kingdom of Jesus, His rule and reign to restore angelic authority in the realms above the earth.

281. I release and declare the Kingdom of Jesus, His rule and reign to cut off communication between fallen watchers and earthly agents.

282. I release and declare the Kingdom of Jesus, His rule and reign to cleanse the sun and moon from every blood ritual and pagan worship.

283. I release and declare the Kingdom of Jesus, His rule and reign to break the power of ancient star worship and zodiac curses.

284. I release and declare the Kingdom of Jesus, His rule and reign to rule over Orion, Pleiades, and every name in the heavens—Jesus is Lord.

285. I release and declare the Kingdom of Jesus, His rule and reign to disrupt all witchcraft calendars governed by celestial movement.

286. I release and declare the Kingdom of Jesus, His rule and reign to remove the names of false gods from the heavens and enthrone Jesus.

287. I release and declare the Kingdom of Jesus, His rule and reign to shift the atmosphere and restore righteous order above the earth.

288. I release and declare the Kingdom of Jesus, His rule and reign to release holy light, prophetic seasons, and signs aligned with redemption.

Section *Fifteen*

Second Heaven and First Heaven (Declarations 289-308)

289. I release and declare the Kingdom of Jesus, His rule and reign over the second heaven—let every demonic throne there be cast down.

290. I release and declare the Kingdom of Jesus, His rule and reign to shatter the demonic network operating in the mid-heaven realm.

291. I release and declare the Kingdom of Jesus, His rule and reign to arrest all monitoring spirits stationed in the second heaven.

292. I release and declare the Kingdom of Jesus, His rule and reign to overrule principalities and powers that operate between earth and heaven.

293. I release and declare the Kingdom of Jesus, His rule and reign to release angelic forces to take dominion in second heaven airspace.

294. I release and declare the Kingdom of Jesus, His rule and reign to dismantle every spiritual stronghold built in the airwaves.

295. I release and declare the Kingdom of Jesus, His rule and reign to silence the command centers of witchcraft, sorcery, and occult warfare.

296. I release and declare the Kingdom of Jesus, His rule and reign to pierce the second heaven with lightning from the throne of God.

297. I release and declare the Kingdom of Jesus, His rule and reign to pull down demonic cloud cover used to block divine revelation.

298. I release and declare the Kingdom of Jesus, His rule and reign to override all satanic resistance to prophetic prayers in the air realm.

299. I release and declare the Kingdom of Jesus, His rule and reign over the first heaven—let the skies above me be open for revelation and rain.

300. I release and declare the Kingdom of Jesus, His rule and reign to destroy altars built by false prophets and witches in low atmospheric realms.

301. I release and declare the Kingdom of Jesus, His rule and reign to strip the enemy of all surveillance technology in the heavens.

302. I release and declare the Kingdom of Jesus, His rule and reign to cleanse the heavens of familiar spirits, psychic powers, and astral forces.

303. I release and declare the Kingdom of Jesus, His rule and reign to close portals opened by rebellion, idolatry, and generational sin.

304. I release and declare the Kingdom of Jesus, His rule and reign to enthrone the Lamb of God above every space between earth and eternity.

305. I release and declare the Kingdom of Jesus, His rule and reign to reign over every principality positioned above regions and territories.

306. I release and declare the Kingdom of Jesus, His rule and reign to purify the heavens with the blood of Jesus and the fire of the Holy Ghost.

307. I release and declare the Kingdom of Jesus, His rule and reign to open the heavens for angelic traffic, prophetic flow, and holy visitation.

308. I release and declare the Kingdom of Jesus, His rule and reign to command all heavenly places to come under subjection to Christ Jesus

JESUS HAS GIVEN YOU ALL AUTHORITY

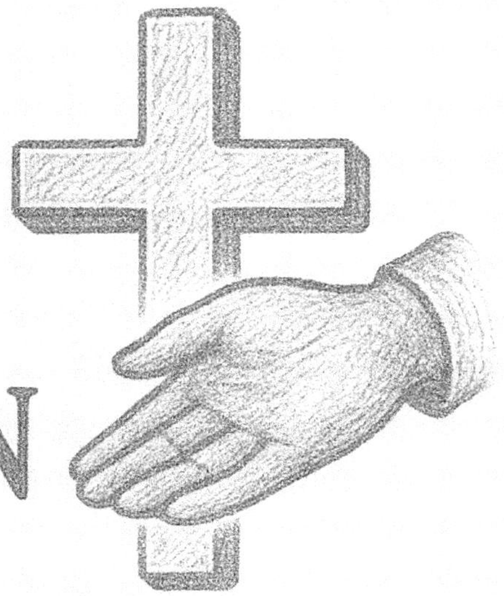

Section Sixteen

The Earth and Land Territories (Declarations 309-328)

309. I release and declare the Kingdom of Jesus, His rule and reign over the earth—let every nation, tribe, and tongue bow to His authority.

310. I release and declare the Kingdom of Jesus, His rule and reign over the land I walk on—let it be cleansed of bloodshed, idolatry, and defilement.

311. I release and declare the Kingdom of Jesus, His rule and reign to shake every ungodly foundation that was laid in rebellion against God.

312. I release and declare the Kingdom of Jesus, His rule and reign to command the soil to produce fruit for the righteous and not for wicked systems.

313. I release and declare the Kingdom of Jesus, His rule and reign over every mountain, hill, and region of influence—let them be inhabited by righteousness.

314. I release and declare the Kingdom of Jesus, His rule and reign over deserts and wildernesses—let them bloom with purpose and promise.

315. I release and declare the Kingdom of Jesus, His rule and reign over the forests and gardens—let creation praise the Lord.

316. I release and declare the Kingdom of Jesus, His rule and reign to expose and destroy territorial spirits operating over cities and nations.

317. I release and declare the Kingdom of Jesus, His rule and reign to cleanse the land from curses spoken by ancestors, witches, or rebels.

318. I release and declare the Kingdom of Jesus, His rule and reign to establish dwelling places of glory throughout the earth.

319. I release and declare the Kingdom of Jesus, His rule and reign to heal the land from environmental destruction and demonic desecration.

320. I release and declare the Kingdom of Jesus, His rule and reign to possess every region with the Gospel of the Kingdom.

321. I release and declare the Kingdom of Jesus, His rule and reign to anoint intercessors to walk the land and reclaim it for Christ.

322. I release and declare the Kingdom of Jesus, His rule and reign to unearth hidden resources, wealth, and provision for Kingdom purposes.

323. I release and declare the Kingdom of Jesus, His rule and reign to drive out ancient spirits of war, bloodshed, and territorial contention.

324. I release and declare the Kingdom of Jesus, His rule and reign to realign geographic boundaries to fulfill prophetic destiny.

325. I release and declare the Kingdom of Jesus, His rule and reign to establish cities of refuge and strongholds of revival across the earth.

326. I release and declare the Kingdom of Jesus, His rule and reign over the dust of the ground—let it no longer respond to curses but to blessings.

327. I release and declare the Kingdom of Jesus, His rule and reign to redeem lands sold in corruption and restore them to Kingdom stewards.

328. I release and declare the Kingdom of Jesus, His rule and reign to make the earth the footstool of Christ and the inheritance of the righteous.

Section Seventeen

The Oceans, Rivers, and Underwater Realms (Declarations 329-348)

329.   I release and declare the Kingdom of Jesus, His rule and reign over every ocean, sea, river, and deep water — let the waters tremble at His voice.

330.   I release and declare the Kingdom of Jesus, His rule and reign to cleanse the waters from blood sacrifices, occult rituals, and marine altars.

331.   I release and declare the Kingdom of Jesus, His rule and reign to break the power of marine spirits, water demons, and Leviathan.

332.   I release and declare the Kingdom of Jesus, His rule and reign to rebuke the winds and waves stirred by demonic tempests and witchcraft.

333.   I release and declare the Kingdom of Jesus, His rule and reign to command the waters to no longer harbor spiritual wickedness or unclean forces.

334.   I release and declare the Kingdom of Jesus, His rule and reign to dismantle thrones of darkness hidden in underwater kingdoms.

335.   I release and declare the Kingdom of Jesus, His rule and reign to expose and destroy hidden wealth, contracts, and pacts stored under the sea.

336.   I release and declare the Kingdom of Jesus, His rule and reign to silence the voices of false prophets who draw power from marine realms.

337.   I release and declare the Kingdom of Jesus, His rule and reign to cleanse the waters from oil spills, toxins, and corruption caused by human greed.

338.   I release and declare the Kingdom of Jesus, His rule and reign over river gates, ocean portals, and submarine canyons — let them glorify the Lord.

339.   I release and declare the Kingdom of Jesus, His rule and reign to break the seductive influence of mermaid spirits and spirits of lust from the sea.

340.   I release and declare the Kingdom of Jesus, His rule and reign to release holy angels to patrol the depths and dismantle underwater covens.

341.   I release and declare the Kingdom of Jesus, His rule and reign to break every generational curse tied to water spirits or coastal rituals.

342.   I release and declare the Kingdom of Jesus, His rule and reign to cause all sea creatures to come under divine order and not serve satanic agendas.

343.   I release and declare the Kingdom of Jesus, His rule and reign to declare dominion over tsunamis, hurricanes, and floods used by darkness.

344.   I release and declare the Kingdom of Jesus, His rule and reign to flood the nations with living water, revelation, and glory.

345.   I release and declare the Kingdom of Jesus, His rule and reign to purify the rivers that feed cities, regions, and spiritual atmospheres.

346.   I release and declare the Kingdom of Jesus, His rule and reign to dismantle hidden witchcraft altars placed in underwater caves.

347.   I release and declare the Kingdom of Jesus, His rule and reign to call the oceans to praise the Lord and yield their harvest to the righteous.

348.   I release and declare the Kingdom of Jesus, His rule and reign to anoint every sea gate and coastal border with angelic fire and protection.

Section Eighteen

The Underworld, Hell, Death, and the Grave (Declarations 349-368)

349. I release and declare the Kingdom of Jesus, His rule and reign over the underworld—let every demonic ruler be dethroned and exposed.

350. I release and declare the Kingdom of Jesus, His rule and reign to cast down spirits of fear, death, and torment rooted in the underworld.

351. I release and declare the Kingdom of Jesus, His rule and reign to shut every gate of hell that wars against the Church and the righteous.

352. I release and declare the Kingdom of Jesus, His rule and reign to break demonic assignments issued from hellish realms and principalities.

353. I release and declare the Kingdom of Jesus, His rule and reign to expose altars built to Hades, Molech, and spirits of sacrifice.

354. I release and declare the Kingdom of Jesus, His rule and reign to cancel every contract made with hell through blood oaths or occult practices.

355. I release and declare the Kingdom of Jesus, His rule and reign to silence every voice speaking from the grave to manipulate the living.

356. I release and declare the Kingdom of Jesus, His rule and reign to reverse every grave-binding and spiritual imprisonment of destinies.

357. I release and declare the Kingdom of Jesus, His rule and reign over cemeteries and burial grounds—let them be sanctified and stripped of demonic residue.

358. I release and declare the Kingdom of Jesus, His rule and reign to release angels to war against necromancy and divination from the dead.

359. I release and declare the Kingdom of Jesus, His rule and reign to destroy every graveyard spirit used to initiate fear, illness, or premature death.

360. I release and declare the Kingdom of Jesus, His rule and reign over death—O death, where is your sting? Christ has conquered you.

361. I release and declare the Kingdom of Jesus, His rule and reign over the grave—O grave, where is your victory? Christ holds the keys.

362. I release and declare the Kingdom of Jesus, His rule and reign to bind spirits of suicide, hopelessness, and the longing for death.

363. I release and declare the Kingdom of Jesus, His rule and reign to command resurrection power over every buried purpose and divine plan.

364. I release and declare the Kingdom of Jesus, His rule and reign to cut off all demonic visitations in dreams from hellish domains.

365. I release and declare the Kingdom of Jesus, His rule and reign to break generational curses tied to ancestors buried under judgment.

366. I release and declare the Kingdom of Jesus, His rule and reign to strip hell of its authority, silence its threats, and exalt Christ alone.

367. I release and declare the Kingdom of Jesus, His rule and reign to establish the banner of victory over every region marked by death and mourning.

368. I release and declare the Kingdom of Jesus, His rule and reign to proclaim the resurrection, the life, and the eternal dominion of Jesus Christ.

Section Nineteen

Principalities, Powers, and Thrones (Declarations 369-388)

369. I release and declare the Kingdom of Jesus, His rule and reign over every principality — let them fall before the throne of Christ.

370. I release and declare the Kingdom of Jesus, His rule and reign to disarm every power and spiritual ruler opposing the Church.

371. I release and declare the Kingdom of Jesus, His rule and reign to expose and destroy hidden rulers of darkness operating through culture and media.

372. I release and declare the Kingdom of Jesus, His rule and reign to shatter strongholds governed by ancient spirits of control, fear, and violence.

373. I release and declare the Kingdom of Jesus, His rule and reign to unseat demonic kings sitting on thrones of corruption in cities and nations.

374. I release and declare the Kingdom of Jesus, His rule and reign to paralyze every power behind generational bondage and ancestral idolatry.

375. I release and declare the Kingdom of Jesus, His rule and reign to bind territorial spirits enforcing crime, addiction, and rebellion.

376. I release and declare the Kingdom of Jesus, His rule and reign to annihilate satanic networks operating through secret societies and occult systems.

377. I release and declare the Kingdom of Jesus, His rule and reign to throw down Jezebel, Leviathan, and every queen of heaven spirit.

378. I release and declare the Kingdom of Jesus, His rule and reign to command the armies of heaven to war against illegal rulers in high places.

379. I release and declare the Kingdom of Jesus, His rule and reign to tear down strongholds that have stood for centuries in resistance to the Gospel.

380. I release and declare the Kingdom of Jesus, His rule and reign to blind the eyes of every demonic watcher and expose their strategies.

381. I release and declare the Kingdom of Jesus, His rule and reign to uproot systems of oppression, manipulation, and religious deception.

382. I release and declare the Kingdom of Jesus, His rule and reign to wage war against witchcraft covens, warlock councils, and satanic prophets.

383. I release and declare the Kingdom of Jesus, His rule and reign to enthrone Christ as King over every gate of society and influence.

384. I release and declare the Kingdom of Jesus, His rule and reign to make the name of Jesus exalted above every dominion, title, and power.

385. I release and declare the Kingdom of Jesus, His rule and reign to nullify all contracts, blood pacts, and thrones not authored by God.

386. I release and declare the Kingdom of Jesus, His rule and reign to flood regions of deep darkness with the radiant light of Christ.

387. I release and declare the Kingdom of Jesus, His rule and reign to usher in revival where strongholds once reigned.

388. I release and declare the Kingdom of Jesus, His rule and reign to fulfill the promise that the kingdoms of this world have become the Kingdom of our God and of His Christ.

Section *Twenty*

Against the Strongman (Declarations 389-403)

389. I release and declare the Kingdom of Jesus, His rule and reign to bind the strongman over my life and house in the name of the Lord.

390. I release and declare the Kingdom of Jesus, His rule and reign to strip the strongman of his armor, influence, and demonic authority.

391. I release and declare the Kingdom of Jesus, His rule and reign to cast the strongman out of my family line and territory.

392. I release and declare the Kingdom of Jesus, His rule and reign to cut off every demonic supply line feeding the strongman.

393. I release and declare the Kingdom of Jesus, His rule and reign to overthrow the strongman assigned to delay my destiny.

394. I release and declare the Kingdom of Jesus, His rule and reign to dethrone every strongman ruling in pride, deception, or fear.

395. I release and declare the Kingdom of Jesus, His rule and reign to silence the voice of the strongman echoing through my bloodline.

396. I release and declare the Kingdom of Jesus, His rule and reign to burn the throne of every territorial strongman with unquenchable fire.

397. I release and declare the Kingdom of Jesus, His rule and reign to render powerless the strongman behind cycles of defeat and infirmity.

398. I release and declare the Kingdom of Jesus, His rule and reign to command the strongman to return what was stolen—sevenfold.

399.   I release and declare the Kingdom of Jesus, His rule and reign to execute judgment written against the strongman in the courts of heaven.

400.   I release and declare the Kingdom of Jesus, His rule and reign to expose every strongman hiding under religious traditions or cultural customs.

401.   I release and declare the Kingdom of Jesus, His rule and reign to break every chain forged by the strongman in dreams or the spirit realm.

402.   I release and declare the Kingdom of Jesus, His rule and reign to plunder the strongman's house and recover every spiritual inheritance.

403.   I release and declare the Kingdom of Jesus, His rule and reign to declare total, public defeat of the strongman before heaven and earth.

Your Breakthrough Is Near

Section Twenty-One

Evil Altars (Declarations 404-418)

404. I release and declare the Kingdom of Jesus, His rule and reign to tear down every evil altar raised against my life, family, and calling.

405. I release and declare the Kingdom of Jesus, His rule and reign to shatter the foundations of altars built by blood, sacrifice, or demonic oaths.

406. I release and declare the Kingdom of Jesus, His rule and reign to desecrate evil altars with the fire of God and the blood of the Lamb.

407. I release and declare the Kingdom of Jesus, His rule and reign to silence the voices crying out from evil altars against my destiny.

408. I release and declare the Kingdom of Jesus, His rule and reign to break covenants, curses, and soul ties activated by demonic shrines.

409. I release and declare the Kingdom of Jesus, His rule and reign to overturn every judgment and decree issued from satanic altars.

410. I release and declare the Kingdom of Jesus, His rule and reign to command the ashes of every evil altar to testify no more.

411. I release and declare the Kingdom of Jesus, His rule and reign to erase my name, family, and bloodline from the records of witchcraft altars.

412. I release and declare the Kingdom of Jesus, His rule and reign to consume with fire every hidden altar buried in the earth or hidden in structures.

413. I release and declare the Kingdom of Jesus, His rule and reign to destroy the priesthoods and intercessors that fuel evil altars.

414. I release and declare the Kingdom of Jesus, His rule and reign to reverse all altar assignments of stagnation, poverty, or barrenness.

415. I release and declare the Kingdom of Jesus, His rule and reign to declare my body, home, and name off-limits to all demonic rituals.

416. I release and declare the Kingdom of Jesus, His rule and reign to scatter the tokens, symbols, and images used to empower evil altars.

417. I release and declare the Kingdom of Jesus, His rule and reign to build the altar of the Lord in my life and family by sacrifice and praise.

418. I release and declare the Kingdom of Jesus, His rule and reign to mark the land where evil altars once stood as holy ground for Kingdom glory.

Section Twenty-Two

Armies of Hell (Declarations 419-433)

419. I release and declare the Kingdom of Jesus, His rule and reign to scatter the armies of hell assigned against my life and city.

420. I release and declare the Kingdom of Jesus, His rule and reign to break the unity and communication lines of every demonic battalion.

421. I release and declare the Kingdom of Jesus, His rule and reign to send confusion into the camps of the armies of darkness.

422. I release and declare the Kingdom of Jesus, His rule and reign to block every reinforcement sent from hell to prolong spiritual warfare.

423. I release and declare the Kingdom of Jesus, His rule and reign to neutralize all weapons formed in the arsenal of hell.

424. I release and declare the Kingdom of Jesus, His rule and reign to blind the scouts and spies sent to monitor Kingdom movement.

425. I release and declare the Kingdom of Jesus, His rule and reign to thunder against every demonic troop marching against my household.

426. I release and declare the Kingdom of Jesus, His rule and reign to burn the banners and flags of satan's armies with holy fire.

427. I release and declare the Kingdom of Jesus, His rule and reign to demolish the demonic war rooms and strategy tables of hell.

428. I release and declare the Kingdom of Jesus, His rule and reign to unleash the angelic hosts of God to destroy satanic formations.

429. I release and declare the Kingdom of Jesus, His rule and reign to arrest generals and commanders in the army of darkness.

430.   I release and declare the Kingdom of Jesus, His rule and reign to dismantle the military ranking systems of demonic government.

431.   I release and declare the Kingdom of Jesus, His rule and reign to silence the war cries of demons, witches, and familiar spirits.

432.   I release and declare the Kingdom of Jesus, His rule and reign to saturate the atmosphere with angelic worship that paralyzes hell.

433.   I release and declare the Kingdom of Jesus, His rule and reign to declare divine victory over every advancing army of darkness.

Section Twenty-Three

Demons and Unclean Spirits (Declarations 434-448)

434. I release and declare the Kingdom of Jesus, His rule and reign to cast out every unclean spirit hiding in my life, family, and environment.

435. I release and declare the Kingdom of Jesus, His rule and reign to expose and drive out demons operating in disguise or religious garments.

436. I release and declare the Kingdom of Jesus, His rule and reign to shut the mouth of every lying spirit sent to deceive and manipulate.

437. I release and declare the Kingdom of Jesus, His rule and reign to command tormenting spirits of fear, anxiety, and restlessness to flee.

438. I release and declare the Kingdom of Jesus, His rule and reign to bind every spirit of infirmity, disease, and lingering affliction.

439. I release and declare the Kingdom of Jesus, His rule and reign to dismantle strongholds built by demons through trauma and abuse.

440. I release and declare the Kingdom of Jesus, His rule and reign to send holy fire into every room and region where unclean spirits dwell.

441. I release and declare the Kingdom of Jesus, His rule and reign to break the legal rights demons claim through sin, ignorance, or inheritance.

442. I release and declare the Kingdom of Jesus, His rule and reign to silence the voices of demons speaking through dreams, thoughts, or people.

443. I release and declare the Kingdom of Jesus, His rule and reign to destroy spiritual parasites and leeching spirits draining energy and strength.

444. I release and declare the Kingdom of Jesus, His rule and reign to sever the cords of soul ties connected to demonic entry points.

445. I release and declare the Kingdom of Jesus, His rule and reign to revoke the assignments of every familiar spirit tracking my movement.

446. I release and declare the Kingdom of Jesus, His rule and reign to evict generational demons from their place of comfort and rest.

447. I release and declare the Kingdom of Jesus, His rule and reign to overturn every demonic throne and idol in my heart and home.

448. I release and declare the Kingdom of Jesus, His rule and reign to flood my soul, body, and atmosphere with purity and deliverance.

Section *Twenty-Four*

Witch Covens and Warlocks (Declarations 449-463)

449. I release and declare the Kingdom of Jesus, His rule and reign to scatter every witch coven operating in my region and sphere.

450. I release and declare the Kingdom of Jesus, His rule and reign to expose every warlock and false prophet working undercover in the Church or community.

451. I release and declare the Kingdom of Jesus, His rule and reign to cancel every spell, incantation, and hex spoken against me and my household.

452. I release and declare the Kingdom of Jesus, His rule and reign to break every blood sacrifice made at midnight or in secret against my life.

453. I release and declare the Kingdom of Jesus, His rule and reign to silence every demonic chant, ritual, or invocation calling my name.

454. I release and declare the Kingdom of Jesus, His rule and reign to shatter the altars of witches and burn their scrolls with holy fire.

455. I release and declare the Kingdom of Jesus, His rule and reign to dismantle demonic assignments and meetings planned in the astral realm.

456. I release and declare the Kingdom of Jesus, His rule and reign to destroy networks of witches and warlocks operating across cities and digital spaces.

457. I release and declare the Kingdom of Jesus, His rule and reign to command confusion and divine division into every occult alliance.

458. I release and declare the Kingdom of Jesus, His rule and reign to tear down spiritual gates opened by witches in families and bloodlines.

459.   I release and declare the Kingdom of Jesus, His rule and reign to remove every surveillance system used by warlocks to monitor Kingdom people.

460.   I release and declare the Kingdom of Jesus, His rule and reign to reverse the effect of potions, charms, and curses released through witchcraft.

461.   I release and declare the Kingdom of Jesus, His rule and reign to blind the eyes of witches seeking to discern or attack me prophetically.

462.   I release and declare the Kingdom of Jesus, His rule and reign to anoint my home, church, and mind as zones off-limits to occult influence.

463.   I release and declare the Kingdom of Jesus, His rule and reign to break every contract made with witches through dreams, agreements, or sins.

Section Twenty-Five

Evil Blood Covenants and Demons in the Bloodline (Declarations 464-478)

464. I release and declare the Kingdom of Jesus, His rule and reign to cancel every evil blood covenant established in my ancestry.

465. I release and declare the Kingdom of Jesus, His rule and reign to sever every demonic pact made by my forefathers knowingly or unknowingly.

466. I release and declare the Kingdom of Jesus, His rule and reign to cleanse my bloodline with the blood of Jesus from the first man to now.

467. I release and declare the Kingdom of Jesus, His rule and reign to silence every demonic voice speaking through bloodline agreements.

468. I release and declare the Kingdom of Jesus, His rule and reign to break curses initiated through blood rituals, sacrifices, and ceremonies.

469. I release and declare the Kingdom of Jesus, His rule and reign to cast out every ancestral demon hiding in my DNA and family tree.

470. I release and declare the Kingdom of Jesus, His rule and reign to block demons from re-entering my life through inherited weaknesses.

471. I release and declare the Kingdom of Jesus, His rule and reign to dismantle generational thrones of wickedness rooted in family altars.

472. I release and declare the Kingdom of Jesus, His rule and reign to reverse every inheritance of shame, loss, or bondage passed through blood.

473. I release and declare the Kingdom of Jesus, His rule and reign to break legal access granted to demons through idolatry in my family line.

474. I release and declare the Kingdom of Jesus, His rule and reign to dissolve every evil dedication made over my life by blood oath.

475. I release and declare the Kingdom of Jesus, His rule and reign to command all bloodline demons to exit my soul, body, and destiny by fire.

476. I release and declare the Kingdom of Jesus, His rule and reign to bring deliverance and liberty to my children and future generations.

477. I release and declare the Kingdom of Jesus, His rule and reign to uproot every evil root planted through generational blood covenants.

478. I release and declare the Kingdom of Jesus, His rule and reign to declare that I am bought by the blood of Jesus — no other blood speaks over me.

Pray Thy Kingdom Come

Section Twenty-Six

Generational Curses and Generational Strongmen (Declarations 479-493)

479. I release and declare the Kingdom of Jesus, His rule and reign to break every generational curse that has ruled in my family line.

480. I release and declare the Kingdom of Jesus, His rule and reign to identify and dismantle the strongman assigned to my bloodline.

481. I release and declare the Kingdom of Jesus, His rule and reign to destroy patterns of sin, addiction, and failure passed through generations.

482. I release and declare the Kingdom of Jesus, His rule and reign to expose curses disguised as personality traits or family traditions.

483. I release and declare the Kingdom of Jesus, His rule and reign to bring to ruin every cycle of poverty, violence, or sickness in my lineage.

484. I release and declare the Kingdom of Jesus, His rule and reign to destroy family spirits operating in secrecy and stubbornness.

485. I release and declare the Kingdom of Jesus, His rule and reign to command every ancient altar in my family line to collapse by fire.

486. I release and declare the Kingdom of Jesus, His rule and reign to silence ancestral voices demanding vengeance or allegiance.

487. I release and declare the Kingdom of Jesus, His rule and reign to cancel every curse spoken by ancestors over future generations.

488. I release and declare the Kingdom of Jesus, His rule and reign to remove the crown of authority from generational strongmen in my family.

489.   I release and declare the Kingdom of Jesus, His rule and reign to revoke covenants made with familiar spirits and guardian demons.

490.   I release and declare the Kingdom of Jesus, His rule and reign to unseat inherited spirits of anger, infirmity, or insanity.

491.   I release and declare the Kingdom of Jesus, His rule and reign to release a new generational legacy of holiness, prosperity, and faith.

492.   I release and declare the Kingdom of Jesus, His rule and reign to command every generational bondage to end with me and not pass on.

493.   I release and declare the Kingdom of Jesus, His rule and reign to redeem my family tree and root it in the bloodline of Christ.

Section Twenty-Seven

Principalities and Powers (Declarations 494-508)

494. I release and declare the Kingdom of Jesus, His rule and reign to tear down every principality ruling over my city, nation, or bloodline.

495. I release and declare the Kingdom of Jesus, His rule and reign to dethrone demonic powers influencing systems of government, education, and media.

496. I release and declare the Kingdom of Jesus, His rule and reign to bind the prince of the power of the air over my region and sphere of influence.

497. I release and declare the Kingdom of Jesus, His rule and reign to strip principalities of their influence over church leadership and doctrine.

498. I release and declare the Kingdom of Jesus, His rule and reign to release divine judgment against territorial spirits ruling through oppression.

499. I release and declare the Kingdom of Jesus, His rule and reign to arrest and exile the strong kings and rulers in high places of wickedness.

500. I release and declare the Kingdom of Jesus, His rule and reign to release warring angels to confront the thrones and dominions of darkness.

501. I release and declare the Kingdom of Jesus, His rule and reign to unmask ancient spirits of deception operating as false light.

502. I release and declare the Kingdom of Jesus, His rule and reign to shatter the crowns and scepters of illegitimate demonic authorities.

503. I release and declare the Kingdom of Jesus, His rule and reign to bind the activity of rulers of darkness over cities and nations.

504.   I release and declare the Kingdom of Jesus, His rule and reign to destroy the veil of blindness cast by principalities over the minds of the lost.

505.   I release and declare the Kingdom of Jesus, His rule and reign to cancel contracts and covenants between earthly kings and demonic powers.

506.   I release and declare the Kingdom of Jesus, His rule and reign to root out corruption fueled by invisible powers behind thrones and seats.

507.   I release and declare the Kingdom of Jesus, His rule and reign to raise up apostolic hubs that dismantle territorial dominion of evil.

508.   I release and declare the Kingdom of Jesus, His rule and reign to exalt Jesus above every name, title, ruler, and dimension.

Section Twenty-Eight

Spiritual Wickedness in High Places (Declarations 509-523)

509. I release and declare the Kingdom of Jesus, His rule and reign to expose every throne of spiritual wickedness operating in high places.

510. I release and declare the Kingdom of Jesus, His rule and reign to strip demonic rulers in politics, media, religion, and finance of their power.

511. I release and declare the Kingdom of Jesus, His rule and reign to confront and scatter wicked spirits that operate through elite systems and global alliances.

512. I release and declare the Kingdom of Jesus, His rule and reign to tear down every pyramid of power built on blood, idolatry, and manipulation.

513. I release and declare the Kingdom of Jesus, His rule and reign to confuse the language and plans of high-level spiritual conspiracies.

514. I release and declare the Kingdom of Jesus, His rule and reign to interrupt every demonic summit, counsel, and meeting held in the spirit realm.

515. I release and declare the Kingdom of Jesus, His rule and reign to command the collapse of demonic towers and strongholds built in spiritual heights.

516. I release and declare the Kingdom of Jesus, His rule and reign to paralyze every satanic agenda working through rulers and influencers.

517. I release and declare the Kingdom of Jesus, His rule and reign to purify the atmosphere of cities and nations from the residue of high-level wickedness.

518. I release and declare the Kingdom of Jesus, His rule and reign to fire divine arrows against the headquarters of spiritual darkness.

519. I release and declare the Kingdom of Jesus, His rule and reign to break enchantments and curses spoken from high places and mountaintops.

520. I release and declare the Kingdom of Jesus, His rule and reign to overturn spiritual structures that exalt themselves against the knowledge of Christ.

521. I release and declare the Kingdom of Jesus, His rule and reign to burn down the high places where idols have been enthroned in hearts and nations.

522. I release and declare the Kingdom of Jesus, His rule and reign to silence the voices of wickedness in thrones, think tanks, and temples.

523. I release and declare the Kingdom of Jesus, His rule and reign to cause the name of Jesus to reign from the highest realm down to the lowest.

Section Twenty-Nine

Over Lives and Cities (Declarations 524-538)

524. I release and declare the Kingdom of Jesus, His rule and reign over my life—let every area submit to His lordship without resistance.

525. I release and declare the Kingdom of Jesus, His rule and reign over my city—let righteousness, justice, and peace be enthroned.

526. I release and declare the Kingdom of Jesus, His rule and reign to overthrow every local altar of crime, violence, and bloodshed.

527. I release and declare the Kingdom of Jesus, His rule and reign to deliver my life from all demonic delays, distractions, and derailments.

528. I release and declare the Kingdom of Jesus, His rule and reign over my mind, habits, and desires—Jesus is King over all.

529. I release and declare the Kingdom of Jesus, His rule and reign to fill my city's gates—media, governance, education—with truth and purity.

530. I release and declare the Kingdom of Jesus, His rule and reign to confront spiritual wickedness hiding behind cultural pride and tradition.

531. I release and declare the Kingdom of Jesus, His rule and reign to raise intercessors, watchmen, and prophets for my neighborhood and city.

532. I release and declare the Kingdom of Jesus, His rule and reign to cleanse the foundations of my life and city from idolatry and injustice.

533. I release and declare the Kingdom of Jesus, His rule and reign to break cycles of generational captivity in communities and families.

534. I release and declare the Kingdom of Jesus, His rule and reign to release healing, revival, and deliverance in every street and household.

535. I release and declare the Kingdom of Jesus, His rule and reign to flood the streets of my city with angelic fire and protection.

536. I release and declare the Kingdom of Jesus, His rule and reign to remove demonic mayors, lawmakers, and influencers who war against truth.

537. I release and declare the Kingdom of Jesus, His rule and reign to enthrone Christ as Lord over every district, institution, and home.

538. I release and declare the Kingdom of Jesus, His rule and reign to fulfill the prophecy: *"The city shall be called The Lord is There."*

Section *Thirty*

False Religion (Declarations 539-553)

539. I release and declare the Kingdom of Jesus, His rule and reign to expose and overthrow every false religion that denies the lordship of Christ.

540. I release and declare the Kingdom of Jesus, His rule and reign to confront every doctrine of demons masquerading as enlightenment.

541. I release and declare the Kingdom of Jesus, His rule and reign to shatter altars built to false gods, idols, and ancestral deities.

542. I release and declare the Kingdom of Jesus, His rule and reign to silence the voice of false prophets leading nations into spiritual adultery.

543. I release and declare the Kingdom of Jesus, His rule and reign to cut off the influence of religions that bind souls in fear, control, and legalism.

544. I release and declare the Kingdom of Jesus, His rule and reign to cancel covenants made with false gods by blood, oath, or culture.

545. I release and declare the Kingdom of Jesus, His rule and reign to remove the veil of blindness caused by religious deception.

546. I release and declare the Kingdom of Jesus, His rule and reign to raise evangelists with authority to dismantle religious strongholds.

547. I release and declare the Kingdom of Jesus, His rule and reign to set captives free from the chains of Islamic, Hindu, Buddhist, and pagan altars.

548. I release and declare the Kingdom of Jesus, His rule and reign to declare that salvation is in no other name but Jesus.

549. I release and declare the Kingdom of Jesus, His rule and reign to tear down sacred texts and rituals exalting lies over truth.

550. I release and declare the Kingdom of Jesus, His rule and reign to burn spiritual bridges connecting generations to false religion.

551. I release and declare the Kingdom of Jesus, His rule and reign to destroy the thrones of false gods in cities and nations.

552. I release and declare the Kingdom of Jesus, His rule and reign to send holy fire into temples of idolatry and deception.

553. I release and declare the Kingdom of Jesus, His rule and reign to proclaim that every knee in every religion shall bow to Christ the King.

YOUR BREAKTHROUGH IS HERE

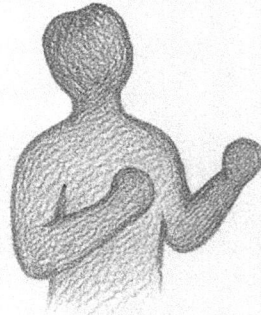

Section Thirty-One

False Teachings and Doctrines (Declarations 554-568)

554. I release and declare the Kingdom of Jesus, His rule and reign to expose every false teaching that leads believers into deception and bondage.

555. I release and declare the Kingdom of Jesus, His rule and reign to overthrow doctrines that deny the cross, the blood, and the resurrection of Christ.

556. I release and declare the Kingdom of Jesus, His rule and reign to bring down every theological system that distorts the nature and character of God.

557. I release and declare the Kingdom of Jesus, His rule and reign to silence every voice that preaches another gospel contrary to the Word of God.

558. I release and declare the Kingdom of Jesus, His rule and reign to correct heresies spoken in pulpits, seminaries, and classrooms around the world.

559. I release and declare the Kingdom of Jesus, His rule and reign to expose the spirit of error operating behind smooth words and enticing doctrines.

560. I release and declare the Kingdom of Jesus, His rule and reign to burn down altars built by false teachers who merchandise the anointing.

561. I release and declare the Kingdom of Jesus, His rule and reign to break the influence of seductive teachings that deny holiness and repentance.

562. I release and declare the Kingdom of Jesus, His rule and reign to cause truth to triumph over every lie taught in the name of religion.

563. I release and declare the Kingdom of Jesus, His rule and reign to dismantle the popularity of false teachers empowered by demonic approval.

564. I release and declare the Kingdom of Jesus, His rule and reign to cleanse the airwaves and digital platforms from theological corruption.

565. I release and declare the Kingdom of Jesus, His rule and reign to restore biblical soundness, apostolic doctrine, and prophetic purity to the Church.

566. I release and declare the Kingdom of Jesus, His rule and reign to bring judgment upon doctrines that enslave rather than liberate.

567. I release and declare the Kingdom of Jesus, His rule and reign to raise up discerning believers who test every spirit and teaching.

568. I release and declare the Kingdom of Jesus, His rule and reign to exalt the Word of God above every tradition and false theology.

Section Thirty-Two

Strongholds of Mind Control (Declarations 569-583)

569. I release and declare the Kingdom of Jesus, His rule and reign to destroy every stronghold of mind control operating in my life and community.

570. I release and declare the Kingdom of Jesus, His rule and reign to sever every neural pathway created by manipulation, trauma, or witchcraft.

571. I release and declare the Kingdom of Jesus, His rule and reign to cast down imaginations and every high thing that exalts itself against the knowledge of God.

572. I release and declare the Kingdom of Jesus, His rule and reign to break the power of media programming and satanic conditioning over the minds of people.

573. I release and declare the Kingdom of Jesus, His rule and reign to unseat demonic voices whispering lies, guilt, and false identities.

574. I release and declare the Kingdom of Jesus, His rule and reign to renew minds by the washing of the Word and the power of truth.

575. I release and declare the Kingdom of Jesus, His rule and reign to disable psychological control systems used by governments, schools, and cults.

576. I release and declare the Kingdom of Jesus, His rule and reign to shut down frequencies of confusion, doubt, and cognitive fog.

577. I release and declare the Kingdom of Jesus, His rule and reign to deliver minds trapped in cycles of shame, fear, and religious bondage.

578. I release and declare the Kingdom of Jesus, His rule and reign to deactivate emotional triggers rooted in past mind control assignments.

579. I release and declare the Kingdom of Jesus, His rule and reign to silence voices of hypnotism, neuro-linguistic programming, and New Age suggestion.

580. I release and declare the Kingdom of Jesus, His rule and reign to rewire my thinking according to Kingdom paradigms and heaven's logic.

531. I release and declare the Kingdom of Jesus, His rule and reign to break every soul tie to teachers, influencers, and leaders who operated in control.

582. I release and declare the Kingdom of Jesus, His rule and reign to call forth prophetic clarity and intellectual liberty.

583. I release and declare the Kingdom of Jesus, His rule and reign to enthrone Christ as the King of my thoughts, imagination, and understanding.

Section *Thirty-Three*

False Churches and Counterfeit Ministries (Declarations 584-598)

584. I release and declare the Kingdom of Jesus, His rule and reign to expose every false church built on greed, control, and deception.

585. I release and declare the Kingdom of Jesus, His rule and reign to uproot ministries that operate in mixture, compromise, and rebellion.

586. I release and declare the Kingdom of Jesus, His rule and reign to reveal wolves in sheep's clothing standing in pulpits of influence.

587. I release and declare the Kingdom of Jesus, His rule and reign to strip titles and mantles from leaders who were not sent by God.

588. I release and declare the Kingdom of Jesus, His rule and reign to bring divine exposure to churches built on charisma without character.

589. I release and declare the Kingdom of Jesus, His rule and reign to cleanse the house of God from every form of merchandising and idolatry.

590. I release and declare the Kingdom of Jesus, His rule and reign to silence voices that preach self, fame, and wealth rather than the cross.

591. I release and declare the Kingdom of Jesus, His rule and reign to tear down every structure where Jezebel and Balaam have been enthroned.

592. I release and declare the Kingdom of Jesus, His rule and reign to bring repentance or removal to those who hinder revival with religion.

593. I release and declare the Kingdom of Jesus, His rule and reign to dry up financial streams flowing to false apostles and teachers.

594. I release and declare the Kingdom of Jesus, His rule and reign to establish apostolic centers built on truth, holiness, and power.

595.   I release and declare the Kingdom of Jesus, His rule and reign to unmask false churches that traffic in false signs and spiritual manipulation.

596.   I release and declare the Kingdom of Jesus, His rule and reign to reform the Church with fire, fear of the Lord, and a return to the Word.

597.   I release and declare the Kingdom of Jesus, His rule and reign to bring divine shaking that separates the wheat from the tares.

598.   I release and declare the Kingdom of Jesus, His rule and reign to declare that Jesus is building His Church, and the gates of hell shall not prevail.

Section *Thirty-Four*

False Gifts and Lying Signs (Declarations 599-613)

599.   I release and declare the Kingdom of Jesus, His rule and reign to expose every false gift operating in the name of the Holy Spirit.

600.   I release and declare the Kingdom of Jesus, His rule and reign to dismantle ministries rooted in counterfeit prophecy, visions, and dreams.

601.   I release and declare the Kingdom of Jesus, His rule and reign to silence familiar spirits mimicking the voice of God.

602.   I release and declare the Kingdom of Jesus, His rule and reign to judge signs and wonders that draw glory to man and not to Christ.

603.   I release and declare the Kingdom of Jesus, His rule and reign to unmask demonic power disguised as healing, revelation, and anointing.

604.   I release and declare the Kingdom of Jesus, His rule and reign to cause lying signs to fail and confuse the sorcerers behind them.

605.   I release and declare the Kingdom of Jesus, His rule and reign to release discernment that tests every spirit and manifestation.

606.   I release and declare the Kingdom of Jesus, His rule and reign to break enchantments and theatrics passed off as spiritual moves.

607.   I release and declare the Kingdom of Jesus, His rule and reign to cast out spirits of divination operating in the Church as prophetic gifts.

608.   I release and declare the Kingdom of Jesus, His rule and reign to cleanse prophetic platforms from manipulation, witchcraft, and flattery.

609.   I release and declare the Kingdom of Jesus, His rule and reign to burn up every false mantle empowered by darkness.

610.   I release and declare the Kingdom of Jesus, His rule and reign to reveal hidden contracts behind those performing counterfeit miracles.

611.   I release and declare the Kingdom of Jesus, His rule and reign to raise up prophets of truth, purity, and holiness in this generation.

612.   I release and declare the Kingdom of Jesus, His rule and reign to protect the Bride from being seduced by signs that lack substance.

613.   I release and declare the Kingdom of Jesus, His rule and reign to exalt the Giver above the gift, the Cross above charisma, and truth above trends.

Section Thirty-Five

Deceptions of the Occult and New Age (Declarations 614-628)

614. (I release and declare the Kingdom of Jesus, His rule and reign to expose and dismantle every New Age deception disguised as enlightenment.

615. I release and declare the Kingdom of Jesus, His rule and reign to break the power of occult practices infiltrating churches, schools, and health systems.

616. I release and declare the Kingdom of Jesus, His rule and reign to burn every hidden symbol, crystal, charm, and token tied to the demonic.

617. I release and declare the Kingdom of Jesus, His rule and reign to silence psychic mediums, spiritualists, and false channels of communication.

618. I release and declare the Kingdom of Jesus, His rule and reign to destroy witchcraft masked as wellness, energy healing, and intuition.

619. I release and declare the Kingdom of Jesus, His rule and reign to break off the fascination with astrology, horoscopes, and zodiac spirits.

620. I release and declare the Kingdom of Jesus, His rule and reign to release truth that exposes lies behind tarot, ancestral reading, and mysticism.

621. I release and declare the Kingdom of Jesus, His rule and reign to blind every watcher spirit seeking to manipulate and mimic revelation.

622. I release and declare the Kingdom of Jesus, His rule and reign to shut down portals opened through meditation, yoga, and false spiritual alignment.

623. I release and declare the Kingdom of Jesus, His rule and reign to tear down New Age philosophies embedded in self-help and motivational doctrines.

624. I release and declare the Kingdom of Jesus, His rule and reign to reclaim those deceived by soul travel, astral projection, and spirit guides.

625. I release and declare the Kingdom of Jesus, His rule and reign to declare Jesus as the only Way, Truth, and Life — there is no other light.

626. I release and declare the Kingdom of Jesus, His rule and reign to scatter New Age covens operating online and through global summits.

627. I release and declare the Kingdom of Jesus, His rule and reign to baptize every seeker of the occult with truth and draw them to repentance.

628. I release and declare the Kingdom of Jesus, His rule and reign to release revival that overtakes New Age movements with power and purity.

Section Thirty-Six

Citywide Pride and Idolatrous Rebellion (Declarations 629-643)

629.   (I release and declare the Kingdom of Jesus, His rule and reign to confront the spirit of pride that governs cities and exalts man above God.

630.   I release and declare the Kingdom of Jesus, His rule and reign to overthrow civic altars built on humanism, self-idolatry, and rebellion.

631.   I release and declare the Kingdom of Jesus, His rule and reign to dismantle towers of pride, perversion, and corruption erected in defiance of truth.

632.   I release and declare the Kingdom of Jesus, His rule and reign to cause the pride of cities to bow before the humility of Christ.

633.   I release and declare the Kingdom of Jesus, His rule and reign to silence political voices that war against the Kingdom through arrogance and lawlessness.

634.   I release and declare the Kingdom of Jesus, His rule and reign to bring repentance and revival to proud institutions that mock the Word of God.

635.   I release and declare the Kingdom of Jesus, His rule and reign to cause the altars of self-worship and cultural pride to collapse.

636.   I release and declare the Kingdom of Jesus, His rule and reign to remove the crowns from heads who refuse to acknowledge the King of Glory.

637.   I release and declare the Kingdom of Jesus, His rule and reign to expose city festivals and public parades rooted in spiritual rebellion.

638.   I release and declare the Kingdom of Jesus, His rule and reign to confront strongholds of pride in education, media, and entertainment.

639.　I release and declare the Kingdom of Jesus, His rule and reign to bring down the lofty gates of rebellion and open the gates of righteousness.

640.　I release and declare the Kingdom of Jesus, His rule and reign to call forth Daniels and Esthers to stand boldly in proud cities.

641.　I release and declare the Kingdom of Jesus, His rule and reign to confront movements built on vanity, self-empowerment, and anti-Christ rhetoric.

642.　I release and declare the Kingdom of Jesus, His rule and reign to flood cities with conviction that births humility and brokenness.

643.　I release and declare the Kingdom of Jesus, His rule and reign to declare that Jesus is Lord over every proud city and its people.

Section Thirty-Seven

Satanic Princes Over Cities (Declarations 644-658)

644. I release and declare the Kingdom of Jesus, His rule and reign to dethrone every satanic prince ruling over my city and its gates.

645. I release and declare the Kingdom of Jesus, His rule and reign to command spiritual eviction of territorial spirits entrenched in urban strongholds.

646. I release and declare the Kingdom of Jesus, His rule and reign to scatter the demonic councils empowering citywide darkness and corruption.

647. I release and declare the Kingdom of Jesus, His rule and reign to dry up the demonic altars feeding satanic princes with blood and sacrifice.

648. I release and declare the Kingdom of Jesus, His rule and reign to silence the decrees of principalities that influence city policies and laws.

649. I release and declare the Kingdom of Jesus, His rule and reign to release the angelic host assigned to war against thrones in high places.

650. I release and declare the Kingdom of Jesus, His rule and reign to break the covenants between civic leaders and demonic principalities.

651. I release and declare the Kingdom of Jesus, His rule and reign to erase spiritual contracts made in darkness on behalf of cities and nations.

652. I release and declare the Kingdom of Jesus, His rule and reign to consume the seat of the serpent in every city center.

653. I release and declare the Kingdom of Jesus, His rule and reign to strip authority from demonic princes cloaked as angels of light.

654. I release and declare the Kingdom of Jesus, His rule and reign to interrupt rituals that empower spiritual rulers with territory and time.

655. I release and declare the Kingdom of Jesus, His rule and reign to declare a prophetic siege against the domain of satanic princes.

656. I release and declare the Kingdom of Jesus, His rule and reign to displace wicked rulers and enthrone the righteousness of Christ in every gate.

657. I release and declare the Kingdom of Jesus, His rule and reign to declare that this city belongs to the Lord and not to Baal or Mammon.

658. I release and declare the Kingdom of Jesus, His rule and reign to declare the fall of every prince of darkness — Jesus alone is King of kings.

Intercession Is the Key

Section Thirty-Eight

Ancestral Worship and Veneration of the Dead (Declarations 659-673)

659.   I release and declare the Kingdom of Jesus, His rule and reign to break every covenant made with ancestral spirits in my bloodline and region.

660.   I release and declare the Kingdom of Jesus, His rule and reign to renounce the worship of the dead and exalt Christ, the only living Mediator.

661.   I release and declare the Kingdom of Jesus, His rule and reign to destroy shrines, altars, and rituals dedicated to deceased ancestors.

662.   I release and declare the Kingdom of Jesus, His rule and reign to silence ancestral voices that demand loyalty, fear, or sacrifice.

663.   I release and declare the Kingdom of Jesus, His rule and reign to deliver entire cultures from the deception of necromancy and ancestral veneration.

664.   I release and declare the Kingdom of Jesus, His rule and reign to redeem family names that have been bound by ancestral worship and blood oaths.

665.   I release and declare the Kingdom of Jesus, His rule and reign to purify homes from inherited items and symbols used in ancestral rites.

666.   I release and declare the Kingdom of Jesus, His rule and reign to declare that the dead do not speak—the voice of Jesus alone gives life.

667.   I release and declare the Kingdom of Jesus, His rule and reign to break spiritual inheritances passed through idolatrous death rituals.

668.   I release and declare the Kingdom of Jesus, His rule and reign to cancel funeral dedications that tied future generations to the dead.

669.   I release and declare the Kingdom of Jesus, His rule and reign to disconnect my soul from every familiar spirit posing as an ancestor.

670.   I release and declare the Kingdom of Jesus, His rule and reign to reverse cultural pride rooted in reverence for ancestral altars.

671.   I release and declare the Kingdom of Jesus, His rule and reign to reclaim nations enslaved by ancestor worship through generations of darkness.

672.   I release and declare the Kingdom of Jesus, His rule and reign to anoint the next generation with revelation, not religion.

673.   I release and declare the Kingdom of Jesus, His rule and reign to exalt the resurrection of Christ over every altar of the dead.

Section Thirty-Nine

Total Victory and Kingdom Possession (Declarations 674-688)

674. I release and declare the Kingdom of Jesus, His rule and reign to possess every gate, region, and realm assigned to the people of God.

675. I release and declare the Kingdom of Jesus, His rule and reign to enforce victory in every battle, whether in the spirit or on earth.

676. I release and declare the Kingdom of Jesus, His rule and reign to bring an end to generational cycles of defeat, delay, and bondage.

677. I release and declare the Kingdom of Jesus, His rule and reign to cause the triumphant Church to rise in purity, power, and dominion.

678. I release and declare the Kingdom of Jesus, His rule and reign to release authority to sons and daughters to rule as priests and kings.

679. I release and declare the Kingdom of Jesus, His rule and reign to activate the full inheritance of the saints in the land of the living.

680. I release and declare the Kingdom of Jesus, His rule and reign to release heavenly blueprints for Kingdom advancement and reformation.

681. I release and declare the Kingdom of Jesus, His rule and reign to seal deliverance with divine occupancy—no enemy shall return.

682. I release and declare the Kingdom of Jesus, His rule and reign to declare that every knee shall bow and every tongue confess His Lordship.

683. I release and declare the Kingdom of Jesus, His rule and reign to plant the banner of Christ in territories once ruled by darkness.

684. I release and declare the Kingdom of Jesus, His rule and reign to rebuild ruined places and raise desolate generations into Kingdom purpose.

685. I release and declare the Kingdom of Jesus, His rule and reign to transform cities into dwelling places of His glory and habitation.

636. I release and declare the Kingdom of Jesus, His rule and reign to execute judgment against darkness and release justice in every sphere.

687. I release and declare the Kingdom of Jesus, His rule and reign to establish divine order where there was chaos, and light where there was darkness.

688. I release and declare the Kingdom of Jesus, His rule and reign to proclaim: "The kingdoms of this world have become the kingdoms of our Lord and of His Christ, and He shall reign forever and ever."

Section Forty

Sexual Perversion and Lifestyles of the Flesh (Declarations 689-703)

689. I release and declare the Kingdom of Jesus, His rule and reign to dismantle every altar of sexual perversion rooted in identity confusion and trauma.

690. I release and declare the Kingdom of Jesus, His rule and reign to break demonic assignments that normalize immorality and glorify fleshly lusts.

691. I release and declare the Kingdom of Jesus, His rule and reign to silence seductive spirits luring generations into sexual rebellion.

692. I release and declare the Kingdom of Jesus, His rule and reign to purify the minds of youth corrupted by media, culture, and compromise.

693. I release and declare the Kingdom of Jesus, His rule and reign to destroy spiritual strongholds behind pornography, masturbation, and deviant fantasies.

694. I release and declare the Kingdom of Jesus, His rule and reign to overturn satanic doctrines that celebrate lust as liberty.

695. I release and declare the Kingdom of Jesus, His rule and reign to cleanse the imagination of every spirit of sensuality and perversion.

696. I release and declare the Kingdom of Jesus, His rule and reign to expose hidden perversion in leadership and call them to repentance or removal.

697. I release and declare the Kingdom of Jesus, His rule and reign to sever soul ties formed through fornication, adultery, and sexual sin.

698. I release and declare the Kingdom of Jesus, His rule and reign to restore purity, innocence, and holiness to broken vessels.

699. I release and declare the Kingdom of Jesus, His rule and reign to judge unrepentant altars of lust in churches, schools, and entertainment.

700. I release and declare the Kingdom of Jesus, His rule and reign to rescue those trapped in lifestyles of shame and silence.

701. I release and declare the Kingdom of Jesus, His rule and reign to empower the Spirit of conviction over compromise and carnality.

702. I release and declare the Kingdom of Jesus, His rule and reign to wash this generation with fire, truth, and deliverance from all sexual bondage.

703. I release and declare the Kingdom of Jesus, His rule and reign to exalt Christ as the model of righteousness above every identity of the flesh.

PRAY THY KINGDOM COME

Section Forty-One

Homosexuality and Lesbianism (Declarations 704-718)

704. I release and declare the Kingdom of Jesus, His rule and reign to tear down the spirit of confusion behind homosexuality and lesbianism.

705. I release and declare the Kingdom of Jesus, His rule and reign to break the lie that identity is found in sexual preference and not in Christ.

706. I release and declare the Kingdom of Jesus, His rule and reign to confront the spirit of pride that celebrates rebellion against divine design.

707. I release and declare the Kingdom of Jesus, His rule and reign to release truth in love that rescues hearts deceived by counterfeit intimacy.

708. I release and declare the Kingdom of Jesus, His rule and reign to cancel generational and emotional wounds that open the door to same-sex attraction.

709. I release and declare the Kingdom of Jesus, His rule and reign to demolish ideologies that normalize sin and silence righteousness.

710. I release and declare the Kingdom of Jesus, His rule and reign to restore purity and identity to those bound by sexual confusion.

711. I release and declare the Kingdom of Jesus, His rule and reign to expose cultural agendas that promote perversion over truth.

712. I release and declare the Kingdom of Jesus, His rule and reign to release bold love that reaches the broken without affirming bondage.

713. I release and declare the Kingdom of Jesus, His rule and reign to remove spiritual blindness that defends behavior contrary to the Word.

714. I release and declare the Kingdom of Jesus, His rule and reign to establish the truth of male and female as designed by the Creator.

715. I release and declare the Kingdom of Jesus, His rule and reign to purify pulpits, classrooms, and media from compromising messages.

716. I release and declare the Kingdom of Jesus, His rule and reign to redeem every testimony corrupted by shame and transform it into deliverance.

717. I release and declare the Kingdom of Jesus, His rule and reign to break spiritual and emotional soul ties formed through same-sex experiences.

718. I release and declare the Kingdom of Jesus, His rule and reign to proclaim the cross of Jesus Christ as the power to transform every identity.

Section Forty-Two

Illicit Drugs and Alcohol Drunkenness (Declarations 719-733)

719. I release and declare the Kingdom of Jesus, His rule and reign to break the chains of addiction to illegal drugs and alcohol.

720. I release and declare the Kingdom of Jesus, His rule and reign to dismantle altars of chemical dependence and generational substance abuse.

721. I release and declare the Kingdom of Jesus, His rule and reign to expose the spirits of escapism and numbness fueling substance addiction.

722. I release and declare the Kingdom of Jesus, His rule and reign to destroy demonic strongholds operating through drug trafficking and distribution.

723. I release and declare the Kingdom of Jesus, His rule and reign to heal emotional trauma and pain that opened the door to addiction.

724. I release and declare the Kingdom of Jesus, His rule and reign to set captives free from the torment of withdrawal, relapse, and shame.

725. I release and declare the Kingdom of Jesus, His rule and reign to deliver minds hijacked by chemical imbalances and hallucinogenic spirits.

726. I release and declare the Kingdom of Jesus, His rule and reign to release fire on every altar where alcohol is worshipped and glorified.

727. I release and declare the Kingdom of Jesus, His rule and reign to release holy hunger to replace the craving for intoxication.

728. I release and declare the Kingdom of Jesus, His rule and reign to reverse the influence of spirits of pharmakeia in cities and youth culture.

729. I release and declare the Kingdom of Jesus, His rule and reign to burn up satanic strategies that use addiction to steal destinies.

730. I release and declare the Kingdom of Jesus, His rule and reign to release divine intervention for those in recovery, detox, and crisis.

731. I release and declare the Kingdom of Jesus, His rule and reign to break shame off the families of addicts and restore generational dignity.

732. I release and declare the Kingdom of Jesus, His rule and reign to cleanse the blood, body, and brain of every chemical residue.

733. I release and declare the Kingdom of Jesus, His rule and reign to proclaim Jesus as the Deliverer from every spirit of bondage and addiction.

Section Forty-Three

Abortion and Shedding of Innocent Blood (Declarations 734-748)

734. I release and declare the Kingdom of Jesus, His rule and reign to confront and dismantle the altar of abortion in my nation.

735. I release and declare the Kingdom of Jesus, His rule and reign to silence the cry of Molech that demands the blood of the innocent.

736. I release and declare the Kingdom of Jesus, His rule and reign to break the covenant between culture and the spirit of death.

737. I release and declare the Kingdom of Jesus, His rule and reign to expose the deception that disguises murder as choice and health care.

738. I release and declare the Kingdom of Jesus, His rule and reign to heal women and men who are bound by guilt, regret, and shame from abortion.

739. I release and declare the Kingdom of Jesus, His rule and reign to revoke blood pacts made through legislation, medicine, and activism.

740. I release and declare the Kingdom of Jesus, His rule and reign to cleanse the land from the blood of children sacrificed to convenience.

741. I release and declare the Kingdom of Jesus, His rule and reign to shut down clinics and operations that profit from bloodshed and fetal trafficking.

742. I release and declare the Kingdom of Jesus, His rule and reign to restore the value of life from the womb to the tomb.

743. I release and declare the Kingdom of Jesus, His rule and reign to raise up voices of truth that contend for the unborn with courage and clarity.

744. I release and declare the Kingdom of Jesus, His rule and reign to bring judgment to unrepentant physicians and lawmakers who shed innocent blood.

745. I release and declare the Kingdom of Jesus, His rule and reign to erase demonic assignments written over the destinies of aborted children.

746. I release and declare the Kingdom of Jesus, His rule and reign to break the influence of global organizations that promote the culture of death.

747. I release and declare the Kingdom of Jesus, His rule and reign to send revival to medical communities and institutions of public health.

748. I release and declare the Kingdom of Jesus, His rule and reign to declare that children are a blessing from the Lord, and not a burden to be eliminated.

Section Forty-Four

Marital Infidelity and Adultery (Declarations 749-763)

749. I release and declare the Kingdom of Jesus, His rule and reign to expose and uproot every spirit of adultery operating in marriages.

750. I release and declare the Kingdom of Jesus, His rule and reign to sever every soul tie formed through emotional or physical betrayal.

751. I release and declare the Kingdom of Jesus, His rule and reign to release the fire of purity over every husband and wife.

752. I release and declare the Kingdom of Jesus, His rule and reign to restore honor, trust, and faithfulness to the covenant of marriage.

753. I release and declare the Kingdom of Jesus, His rule and reign to dismantle lust-driven fantasies and relationships that threaten covenant.

754. I release and declare the Kingdom of Jesus, His rule and reign to burn up every altar of infidelity built in secret and in darkness.

755. I release and declare the Kingdom of Jesus, His rule and reign to bring deep repentance and divine counsel where betrayal has occurred.

756. I release and declare the Kingdom of Jesus, His rule and reign to remove seducing spirits sent to divide marriages through manipulation and flattery.

757. I release and declare the Kingdom of Jesus, His rule and reign to restore intimacy and fidelity between spouses under spiritual attack.

758. I release and declare the Kingdom of Jesus, His rule and reign to redeem broken homes and repair the breach caused by infidelity.

759. I release and declare the Kingdom of Jesus, His rule and reign to silence demonic lies that say covenant is outdated or unnecessary.

760. I release and declare the Kingdom of Jesus, His rule and reign to bind the wandering eye and awaken the heart to covenant love.

761. I release and declare the Kingdom of Jesus, His rule and reign to uproot generational curses of adultery and divorce in family lines.

762. I release and declare the Kingdom of Jesus, His rule and reign to discipline leaders who model unfaithfulness in their private lives.

763. I release and declare the Kingdom of Jesus, His rule and reign to proclaim that what God has joined together, no demon shall divide.

Section Forty-Five

Child Abuse and Paedophilia (Declarations 764-778)

764. I release and declare the Kingdom of Jesus, His rule and reign to expose every hidden act of child abuse and pedophilia in homes, churches, and systems.

765. I release and declare the Kingdom of Jesus, His rule and reign to bring divine justice to predators and traffickers who prey on innocent children.

766. I release and declare the Kingdom of Jesus, His rule and reign to break spiritual covenants that protect pedophiles and institutional abusers.

767. I release and declare the Kingdom of Jesus, His rule and reign to cleanse every child's soul from the trauma, fear, and torment of abuse.

768. I release and declare the Kingdom of Jesus, His rule and reign to destroy demonic networks that traffic and exploit children globally.

769. I release and declare the Kingdom of Jesus, His rule and reign to release angels of protection over vulnerable children in every nation.

770. I release and declare the Kingdom of Jesus, His rule and reign to raise up holy guardians and deliverers for this generation's youth.

771. I release and declare the Kingdom of Jesus, His rule and reign to silence the voice of manipulation used to keep abuse hidden.

772. I release and declare the Kingdom of Jesus, His rule and reign to expose satanic rituals, covens, and circles that use children as sacrifices.

773. I release and declare the Kingdom of Jesus, His rule and reign to break the power of childhood molestation from shaping adult identities.

774. I release and declare the Kingdom of Jesus, His rule and reign to purify every institution—from orphanages to schools—from hidden predators.

775. I release and declare the Kingdom of Jesus, His rule and reign to release psychological and emotional healing to adult survivors of childhood abuse.

776. I release and declare the Kingdom of Jesus, His rule and reign to burn the demonic blueprint that seeks to normalize pedophilia in society.

777. I release and declare the Kingdom of Jesus, His rule and reign to restore joy, innocence, and safety to childhood in every city.

778. I release and declare the Kingdom of Jesus, His rule and reign to declare that children are arrows in the hands of the righteous—safe, protected, and anointed.

Section Forty-Six

Murder and Spirits of Bloodshed (Declarations 779-793)

779.   I release and declare the Kingdom of Jesus, His rule and reign to expose and dismantle the spirit of murder operating in families, cities, and nations.

780.   I release and declare the Kingdom of Jesus, His rule and reign to break demonic rage and violence that leads to premeditated and impulsive killing.

781.   I release and declare the Kingdom of Jesus, His rule and reign to judge unrepentant hands that shed innocent blood for power, vengeance, or profit.

782.   I release and declare the Kingdom of Jesus, His rule and reign to silence the cry of the avenger and release the voice of mercy and repentance.

783.   I release and declare the Kingdom of Jesus, His rule and reign to disrupt plots of mass violence, domestic terrorism, and public bloodshed.

784.   I release and declare the Kingdom of Jesus, His rule and reign to scatter every altar where blood sacrifices fuel demonic covenants.

785.   I release and declare the Kingdom of Jesus, His rule and reign to remove assassins and killers who traffic in death under legal or spiritual cover.

786.   I release and declare the Kingdom of Jesus, His rule and reign to disarm neighborhoods and nations held captive by gang warfare and genocide.

787.   I release and declare the Kingdom of Jesus, His rule and reign to deliver families bound by generational blood feuds and revenge killings.

788.   I release and declare the Kingdom of Jesus, His rule and reign to cancel every murderous assignment spoken, written, or planned in darkness.

789. I release and declare the Kingdom of Jesus, His rule and reign to bring peace to blood-stained streets, cities, and regions once ruled by violence.

790. I release and declare the Kingdom of Jesus, His rule and reign to uproot the political and spiritual thrones of those who profit from death.

791. I release and declare the Kingdom of Jesus, His rule and reign to raise up intercessors who intercept murder through prophetic authority.

792. I release and declare the Kingdom of Jesus, His rule and reign to declare that the blood of Jesus speaks louder than the blood of Abel.

793. I release and declare the Kingdom of Jesus, His rule and reign to turn the hearts of murderers into redeemed sons and daughters.

Section Forty-Seven

Wicked Thoughts and Corrupt Imaginations (Declarations 794-808)

794. I release and declare the Kingdom of Jesus, His rule and reign to cast down every vain imagination that exalts itself against the knowledge of God.

795. I release and declare the Kingdom of Jesus, His rule and reign to purify the thought life of every believer polluted by darkness and deception.

796. I release and declare the Kingdom of Jesus, His rule and reign to bind mind-invading spirits that implant wicked fantasies and evil meditations.

797. I release and declare the Kingdom of Jesus, His rule and reign to cleanse the inner dialogue of doubt, fear, lust, violence, and pride.

798. I release and declare the Kingdom of Jesus, His rule and reign to renew the minds of a generation raised on digital corruption and mental chaos.

799. I release and declare the Kingdom of Jesus, His rule and reign to demolish mental strongholds that fuel addictions, rebellion, and perversion.

800. I release and declare the Kingdom of Jesus, His rule and reign to bring the mind into obedience to Christ and the truth of His Word.

801. I release and declare the Kingdom of Jesus, His rule and reign to arrest imaginations that glorify evil, bloodshed, and false power.

802. I release and declare the Kingdom of Jesus, His rule and reign to silence inner tormentors that replay sin, abuse, and failure.

803. I release and declare the Kingdom of Jesus, His rule and reign to break false visualizations and manifestations rooted in occult mind practices.

804. I release and declare the Kingdom of Jesus, His rule and reign to remove daydreams and night visions inspired by unclean spirits.

805. I release and declare the Kingdom of Jesus, His rule and reign to shut off access points in the mind that give entry to enemy suggestions.

806. I release and declare the Kingdom of Jesus, His rule and reign to wash every mental altar with the blood of Jesus and the water of the Word.

807. I release and declare the Kingdom of Jesus, His rule and reign to sanctify imagination for prophetic creativity and divine insight.

808. I release and declare the Kingdom of Jesus, His rule and reign to proclaim the mind of Christ over every thought, pattern, and intention.

Section Forty-Eight

Sickness, Infirmity, and Disease (Declarations 809-823)

809. I release and declare the Kingdom of Jesus, His rule and reign to overthrow every spirit of infirmity afflicting the bodies of God's people.

810. I release and declare the Kingdom of Jesus, His rule and reign to cancel every generational curse of sickness and inherited disease.

811. I release and declare the Kingdom of Jesus, His rule and reign to rebuke the spirits behind chronic illness, fatigue, and mystery conditions.

812. I release and declare the Kingdom of Jesus, His rule and reign to burn up every demonic altar of affliction established through witchcraft or bloodline sin.

813. I release and declare the Kingdom of Jesus, His rule and reign to command every organ, system, and cell in the body to come into divine alignment.

814. I release and declare the Kingdom of Jesus, His rule and reign to destroy the legal rights of affliction rooted in unrepented sin and trauma.

815. I release and declare the Kingdom of Jesus, His rule and reign to rebuke cancer, autoimmune diseases, viruses, and infections by the blood of Jesus.

816. I release and declare the Kingdom of Jesus, His rule and reign to restore creative miracles to limbs, bones, nerves, and the brain.

817.   I release and declare the Kingdom of Jesus, His rule and reign to release healing angels assigned to bodies under demonic attack.

818.   I release and declare the Kingdom of Jesus, His rule and reign to break spiritual assignments behind premature death and medical misdiagnosis.

819.   I release and declare the Kingdom of Jesus, His rule and reign to cleanse hospitals, clinics, and homes with the healing glory of God.

820.   I release and declare the Kingdom of Jesus, His rule and reign to expose pharmakeia—sorcery through drugs and false healing practices.

821.   I release and declare the Kingdom of Jesus, His rule and reign to reverse the sentence of terminal illness and speak resurrection life.

822.   I release and declare the Kingdom of Jesus, His rule and reign to activate the gift of healing and the working of miracles in the Body of Christ.

823.   I release and declare the Kingdom of Jesus, His rule and reign to proclaim that by His stripes we are healed—spirit, soul, and body.

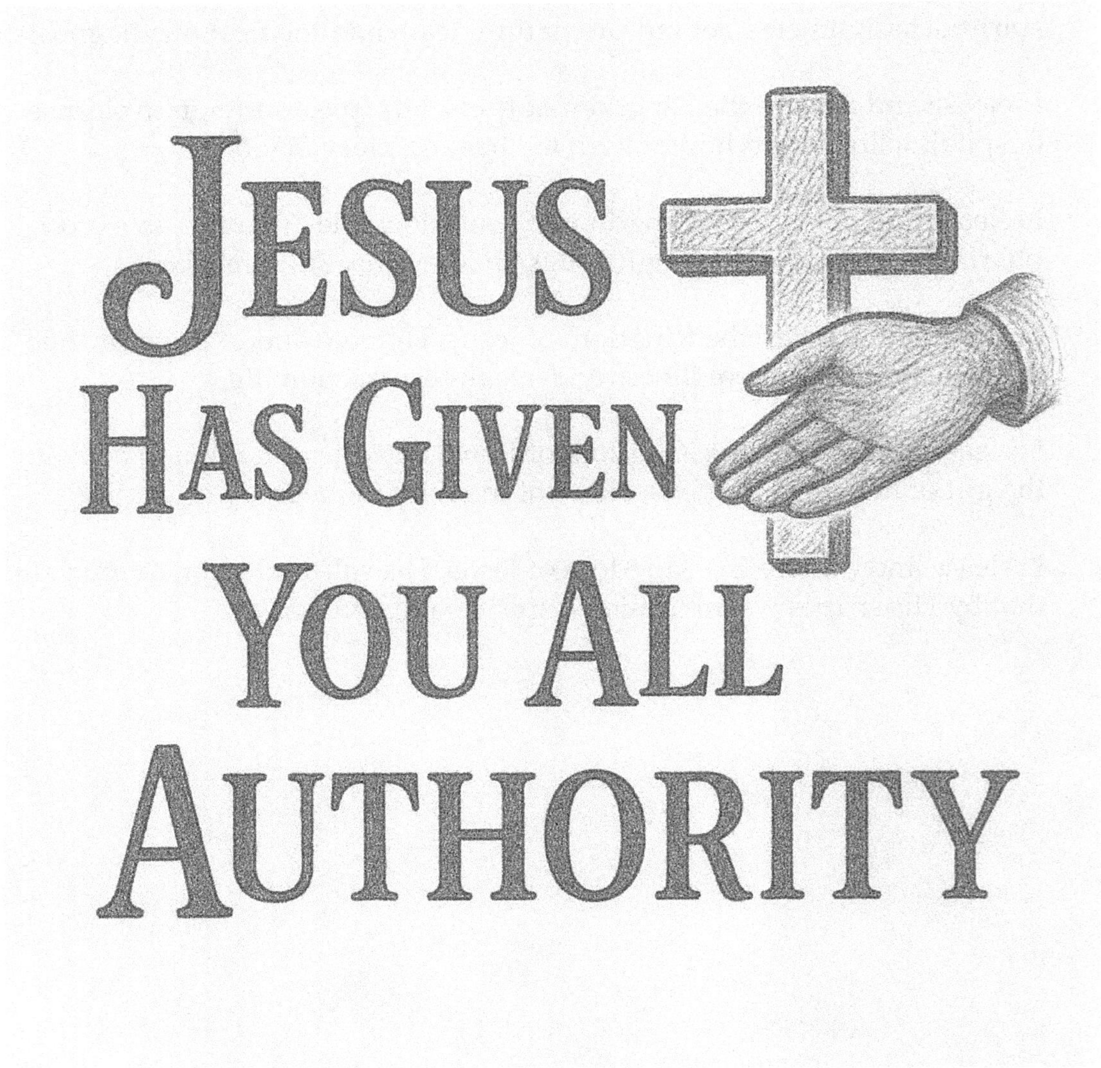
JESUS
HAS GIVEN
YOU ALL
AUTHORITY

Section Forty-Nine

Victory Over Death and the Grave (Declarations 824-838)

824. I release and declare the Kingdom of Jesus, His rule and reign to rebuke the spirit of premature death and every assignment of the grave.

825. I release and declare the Kingdom of Jesus, His rule and reign to destroy fear of death and replace it with hope in eternal life.

826. I release and declare the Kingdom of Jesus, His rule and reign to dismantle covenants made with death through words, rituals, or bloodlines.

827. I release and declare the Kingdom of Jesus, His rule and reign to resurrect destinies buried by grief, trauma, or demonic plots.

828. I release and declare the Kingdom of Jesus, His rule and reign to break every sentence of spiritual death pronounced over lives, ministries, and callings.

829. I release and declare the Kingdom of Jesus, His rule and reign to silence voices from the grave calling people back into bondage and sorrow.

830. I release and declare the Kingdom of Jesus, His rule and reign to reveal Christ's victory over the final enemy — death itself.

831. I release and declare the Kingdom of Jesus, His rule and reign to burn up every death ritual rooted in ancestral worship, witchcraft, or occultism.

832. I release and declare the Kingdom of Jesus, His rule and reign to close every gate of Sheol opened by sin, unbelief, or spiritual ignorance.

833. I release and declare the Kingdom of Jesus, His rule and reign to call back to life every Lazarus tied by grave clothes of despair and hopelessness.

834. I release and declare the Kingdom of Jesus, His rule and reign to abolish fear-based doctrines that glorify death over resurrection.

835. I release and declare the Kingdom of Jesus, His rule and reign to reverse curses of dying young, tragic endings, and untimely demise.

836. I release and declare the Kingdom of Jesus, His rule and reign to release angelic intervention in moments of near death or spiritual transition.

837. I release and declare the Kingdom of Jesus, His rule and reign to proclaim the keys of death and the grave now belong to Christ alone.

838. I release and declare the Kingdom of Jesus, His rule and reign to declare that life, and life more abundantly, is our portion through Jesus Christ.

You are a warrior. You are a vessel of dominion. You are a threat to hell.

Go forth in the name of the Lord Jesus — the Captain of the Hosts — and possess the gates of the enemy.

Victory is not just your portion — it is your calling.

More Books By

Dr. Kelafo and Shallaywa Collie

— Go Global Leadership Keys: Strategies for Your Business, Brand and Organization to Have Global Impact

— You are my Father; I am your Son - Understanding Kingdom Sonship (Revised)

— A Lifetime Relationship: Life Building Time in the Presence of God, 52 Week Devotional for Men and Women

— Victory: 21 Powerful, Prayerful Biblical Declarations to Begin Your Day

— Heavenly Prayers to Live Inspired, Empowered and Fulfilled Daily (Revised)

— Practical Keys to Knowing Christ to Walk in Deliverance, Purpose and Destiny (Revised)

— The Kingdom: Experience Heaven on Earth

— The Kingdom: Experience Heaven on Earth Part II

— The Power Experience Heaven's Authority

— Healthy Smoothies: Vibrant and Wholesome Recipes for a Healthy You

— Nourish and Thrive: Fuel Your Body Right- Wholesome Delights with Keto Inspirations

— The Glory: Experience Heaven's Wealth

— Women in the Presence of God: Fashioned for the Kingdom of God

— Women in the Prescence of God - Fashioned for the Kingdom of God: Companion Notebook Capture Your Blissfully Happy Thoughts

— The Royal Teachings & Decrees of King Jesus: His Answers to Everyone's Questions

— Apostolic Christian Foundation: Rediscovering Apostolic Christianity and The Kingdom of God and The foundational Doctrine Every Believer Should Know

Available on www.Amazon.com | www.kingdomtrilogy.com

**For more materials, to connect with and book
Dr. Kelafo and Shallaywa Collie, visit
and subscribe to these platforms:**

www.kamgbahamas.com
www.kelafozcollie.com
www.shallaywa.com
www.majesticpriesthoodpublications.com
YouTube: Kami Bahamas

About the Book

"Praying the Kingdom of Jesus – Apostolic Declarations for Spiritual Dominion" is a bold, unprecedented prayer manual composed of over **750 authoritative declarations**, organized in strategic sections targeting the greatest spiritual battles of our time.

The declarations begin with the heart and mind — areas where identity, desire, willpower, and emotional bondage reside. They expand into marriages, families, education, business, medicine, entertainment, media, and government. From there, they ascend into heavenly warfare over the sun, moon, stars, and second heaven, descend into realms of darkness including the underworld and death, and pierce through every false altar, demonic contract, and counterfeit religion. Each section builds spiritual momentum, activating the royal authority of Jesus through the spoken word.

Grounded in Scripture and shaped by Apostolic and Prophetic theology, this work carries the literary intensity of **Kingdom, warfare and revelatory structure,** and the urgency of modern-day watchmen. Every declaration is framed with one unshakable thesis:

"I release and declare the Kingdom of Jesus, His rule and reign..."

This phrase is more than a statement — it is a legal invocation, a governmental release of heaven's authority to confront hell's agenda. Each declaration enforces spiritual sovereignty in areas the enemy has long occupied: sexual immorality, drug addiction, mental torment, cultural rebellion, religious deception, spiritual complacency, and generational curses.

Additionally with spiritual precision and prophetic clarity, this work tears down strongholds of, ancestral worship, perversion, murder, idolatry, and witchcraft — and enforces the redemptive, righteous dominion of King Jesus.

This book serves as:

- A **war manual** for deliverance ministers

- A **curriculum** for schools of prayer and intercession

- A **breakthrough journal** for personal and corporate transformation

This apostolic decree manual is an essential tool for:

- Apostolic leaders and prophetic hubs

- Intercessory prayer teams

- Revival centers and ministry schools

- Deliverance ministries and Kingdom hubs

- Individual believers seeking divine breakthrough

About the Authors

Dr. Kelafo Collie, is a distinguished Medical Physician, Apostolic Leader, and founder of **Kingdom Apostolic Ministries International and Kingdom Apostolic Global Networks**. Alongside his wife, **Dr. Shallaywa Collie**, a Scholar, Teacher, and Global Influencer, they have pioneered an international movement of Kingdom transformation.

Together, they are:

- **Doctor of Divinity**, authors of over **20 books** on Spiritual Authority, Prayer, Healing, and Kingdom Living

- **Global Leaders** with a mandate to teach and preach the Kingdom of Jesus in every nation

- **Hosts of Power and Glory TV**, a global television network broadcasting the Gospel of the Kingdom

- **Overseers of Kingdom Apostolic Global Network**, uniting churches and ministries under Apostolic covering

- **Founders of Ralpha Health Center**, a prophetic model of Kingdom Healthcare transformation

- **Advisors to government officials, private industry leaders, and corporate institutions worldwide**

- **Proud parents** of two biological children and **spiritual parents** to many sons and daughters around the world

They are known as **pioneering Prayer Generals, Kingdom reformers**, and **prophetic voices** in this generation. Their passion is to **empower the Body of Christ**, restore Apostolic order, and raise up a global army of spiritual warriors who enforce heaven's rule in the earth.

The Whole Earth is Filled with His Glory

www.ingramcontent.com/pod-product-compliance
Lightning Source LLC
Chambersburg PA
CBHW052331100426
42737CB00055B/3307